Social Responsibilities of Technologists, Scientists and Managers

Edited by :
Anuradha Sharma
and
Raka Sharan

GIAN PUBLISHING HOUSE
NEW DELHI

GIAN PUBLISHING HOUSE
4-C Ansari Road, Daryaganj
New Delhi—110002

ISBN 81—212—0331—7

PRINTED IN INDIA

Published by Mrs. Gayatri Garg for Gian Publishing House, New Delhi 110002. and Printed at Godwall Printers, Delhi.

Preface

'Social responsibility of scientists, technologists and managers' has been the foremost concern of great scientists and social thinkers for many years and this has often been debated through various perspectives. This book highlights development, survival and growth of organisation and society through auditing, monitoring and forecasting of the impacts of scientific and technological developments and managerial assumptions. In fact, knowledge about technological analysis remains incomplete without understanding its effects on people. This book is an attempt in this direction. Based on the contributions of scientists, technologists and administrators, this book brings out the socio-technical concerns for development. Like many other books on the subject, this book does not take a negative and survival perspective. The set of ideas presented are neutral, developmental, analytical and systems oriented. It presents a deep concern for value system analysis.

Social responsibility is still considered a fringe activity by average scientists and technologists. Perhaps that is the reason for no serious and systematic attempts to define the concept.

John Hargreaves and Jan Dauman in their book *Business Survival and Socal Changes* (Associated Business Programme, 1975, London) proposed two definitions of social responsibility. The first is that any organization has a responsibility for planning and managing its relationships with

all those involved in or affected by its activities or with those who, in turn, can affect the ability of the organization to operate effectively and achieve objectives. In the second definition they say that social responsibility is the anticipated, planned and arranged response of our organization to social and political change. The theme of management of change is thus fundamental in the concept of social responsibility. From the above classification and definition of the concept it becomes clear that social responsibility is an important part of the total system and cannot be regarded as just a fringe activity.

This book mainly concentrates on the concept from the point of view of science and technology. The ideas of this book are presented under groups of 'macro' and 'micro' issues. The individual and organizational concerns are generally classified as 'micro' perspective and societal concerns in general are included in the 'macro' perspective.

Fundamentally, an effort has been made to draw attention of technical education planners, and policy makers towards a newer perspective of technical education. It is argued that the education system must be designed to impart awareness and preparedness to face challenges of social change.

Anuradha Sharma and
Raka Sharan

Editrioal Note

In the recent years there has been a growing realization that no technology can sustain itself for long without adequate design within systems perspective. Society and human beings are important subsystems of a technological system. Various aspects of 'Science—Technology—Society' phenomenon, thus include ecological, psychological, sociological, political, managerial, commercial and economic correlates. Issues of this nature with human side of science and technology constitute the subject matter of social responsibility of technologists, scientists, and managers. The new paradigm of socio-technical approach is the grand framework of various social science applications emphasizing on continuous interaction of technological world and human needs. Human side of science and technology is the inevitable concern of today's technological age and needs to be integrated in the educational system as well.

A few years ago, some discussions were held at various technical institutions on Engineering educations. These discussions pointed out that technologists should not only possess a sound grasp of mathematics, science fundamentals, the principles of engineering design but they must develop a good understanding of cultural and human values and some awareness towards the social context of science and technology. In the similar vein, the larger social context also should be able to appreciate its responsibility towards scientists and technologists. To generate some debate on this issue the

Indian Institute of Technology, Delhi organised under a workshop under the auspices of curriculum development programme covering a wide range of ideas. The present volume is the outcome of this workshop. The participants were from the Indian Institutes of Technology, Universities, research organisations and administration and industrial units. The enlargement of social context component was seen at the base-level of technical education. It was felt that engineers, scientists and managers are lacking in this aspect and they should be trained to become more aware of their responsibilities toward the larger social context.

It is well known that modern scientists and technologists would have to shoulder much more responsibilities than their predecessors. Thus, they require technical excellence with a greater understanding of the non-technical consequences of technical advances. They have to be fully conversant with the result of socio-technical factors. The present volume is a modest attempt in this direction.

The domain of social responsibility of *scientists, technologists* and *managers* is divided into two parts with macro and micro perspectives in this book. Macro perspective starts with the keynote address of Prof. S. Sampath, Director, Defence Research and Development Organisation as the first paper. This section presents thirteen papers on broader issues of the subject. Prof. J.N. Kapoor, Dr. T.S. Ananthu and Dr. Pankaj Sharan have highlighted the impact of cultural values and beliefs on the growth of science and technology. Prof. Kapoor emphasises on the role a scientist or technologist has to play in selling a role model by his/her objectivity, reasoning and honesty. Expressing his views on 'Beyond Intellect' Dr. Ananthu says that the foundations of science need to be modified to enable the 'incorporation' of 'mystic' or 'inner work' processes *i.e.* those methods by which we can raise our standards of functioning as human beings, become more humane, more humble, more considerate and more loving. Dr. Pankaj Sharan's paper stresses on the role of predominant values and beliefs on development of science. In the context of curriculum of technologists and scientists, Prof. V.N. Arora recommends increased inputs of non-utilization courses

termed 'useless' according to present value system to make them better humans along with better technologists. Prof. P.L. Dhar and Prof. R.R. Gaur point out that in the changed time and context, after Industrial Revolution, new meaning for the words 'development' and 'welfare' need to be developed. In the present context economic perspective domainates the meaning of development totally disregarding other aspects. They stress that today's technologists must be trained to distinguish between 'good' and 'pleasant' technologies vis-a-vis 'welfare'. Prof. Satsangi describes the three dimensional framework of Hall, with dimension of time, logic and knowledge. Listing four components of programme planning, he emphasizes on the methodology for value system design while role and responsibilities of bureaucrats are highlighted in the paper 'The Indian Bureaucracy : Role Responsibilities and Constrints' written by Nivedita P. Haran and Raka Sharan. This paper has given some fruitful suggestions for the Indian bureaucracy to make it more efficient and performance oriented.

In the paper entitled 'Technology and Development Beneficiary Oriented Approach' Prof. Vasudeven, Dr. Santosh and Dr. Gujral once again raise the question as to whose welfare technology is for. Talking about material aspects of development they urge that technologists must keep in mind the value system of those who benefit from it and issues of equity are sustainability and need fulfilment of masses. They also suggest that training of technologist in the area of technology assessment is necessary.

Prof. Iqbal Khan and Ms. Iqbal suggest that course curriculum for future engineers should focus on leadership qualities and such factors in addition to technical competence since tomorrow's technocrats need to be trained and groomed to attain appreciation of human factors and society's expectations. Dr. Haribabu highlights the economic and political dimensions of pollution and stresses that there is need for political action to protect environment. He suggests that courses must be designed to bring awareness among students about this aspect of technological development.

Part II of the volume presents a micro perspective of Social

responsibility of technologists, scientists and managers. There are seven issues dealt with in this section.

Dr. Lila Krishnan points out that one of the responsibilities that scientists, technologists and managers have towards society is that of communication information that would further the interests of society. She highlights certain issues pertaining to communication strategies which optionally fulfil social responsibilities.

Emphasising on wastivity as a social responsibility Dr. Sushil points out that growing urbanization and industrialization create new challenges for waste management. This complex issue has serious sociological, ecological and economic implications. He observes that a sustained effort is needed to restore the socio-psychological balance of nature in order to optimally harness the available resources.

Dr. V. Upadhyay talks about inadequate laws and measures to protect the entity called 'Consumer' which cuts across all professions, disciplines and ages. He states that scientists and technologists can aid consumer protection by developing tests to ensure quality. As MRTP law has extended its scope to educational institutions recently, we in educational institutions have to be cautious about the quality of education imparted. He observes that the prospects of drawing a parallel of an educational institution with an industrial house may not be pleasant, but at times conforms to our experience as parents.

Commenting on the causes of major industrial accidents, Dr. Raka Sharan suggested that one should learn from such accidents and mechanisms must be created to prevent the occurrence of similar accidents in future. The assessment of social responsibility of an industrial venture must consider the issues from the perspective of participants in the system including the victims of disasters.

Dr. Sabita Karunesh highlights the social responsibility of organizations in terms of emotional and social factors leading to stress, frustration tardiness, friction lowered performance, grievances, absenteeism, alcoholism and accidents. Since these problems have tremendous impact on the members of

society, mental health perspective of organizational designs must be considered.

Talking about modern technology and their impact on human lives, Dr. Anuradha Sharma proposed that the work designs should not be technologically deterministic but must permit enrichment. Analysing the case of computer technology she argues that the technology should move in the direction which provides maximum gains for society.

In the last chapter, views of some other experts have been compiled on 'perspectives on social responsibility of managers'. These include the views of Dr. A.L. Agrawal on multiple role of engineering professionals, Dr. Amulya Khurana's views on 'managerial communication', Dr. Banwet's views of quality of life and quality of work life, Dr. Jain's views on promotion of researches and academic administration, Dr. M.C. Mathur's views on public systems methodology and Mr. Arumugham's views on technological systems and management of change.

The key questions in the social responsibility of scientists, technologists and managers are raised in the last section of the book which need to be deliberated upon and debated.

We thank the curriculum development cell, Department of Electrical Engineering, Indian Institute of Technology, Delhi for making financial grants available for the workshop on which this book is based. Thanks are also due to all the participants of the workshop and the contributors to this volume for their valuable contributions.

Thanks are also due to M/s. Gian Publishing House, New Delhi for undertaking the publication of this book and bringing out the book expeditiously. Finally, although this volume covers reasonably large number of topics related to the theme, we do not claim to present the coverage of all the perspectives. We, however, hope that the views brought out through this book will be useful for decision-makers, planners, students politicians, industrial and teachers alike.

Anuradha Sharma and
Raka Sharan

Contributors

Prof. S. Sampath	Director, R.A.C. Defence Research and Development Organisation, Ministry of Defence, Government of India New Delhi.
Prof. J.N. Kapoor	Emeritus Professor, University Grants Commission, New Delhi.
Dr. T. S. Ananthu	Gandhi Peace Foundation New Delhi.
Dr. Pankaj Sharan	Department of Physics Iamia Milla Islamia New Delhi-110 025.
Prof. V.N. Arora	Department of Humanities and Social Sciences Indian Institute of Technology, Delhi-110016.
Prof. P.L. Dhar	Department of Mechanical Engineering Indian Institute of Technology, Delhi-110016.
Dr. R.R. Gaur	Department of Mechanical Engineering Indian Institute of Technology, Delhi-110016.

Prof. P.S. Satsangi	Department of Electrical Engineering, Indian Institute of Technology Delhi-110016.
Ms. Nivedita Haran, IAS	Depaty Secretary, Department of Personnel Govt. of India, New Delhi.
Dr. Raka Sharan	Department of Humanities and Social Sciences, Indian Institute of Technology Delhi-110016.
Mr. Amalendu Shekhar	Research Scholar, Department of Humanities and Social Sciences, Indian Institute of Technology Delhi-110016.
Prof. Padma Vasudevan	Centre for Rural Development and Appropriate Technology Indian Institute of Technology Delhi-110016.
Dr. Santosh	Centre for Rural Development and Appropriate Technology India Institute of Technology Delhi-110016.
Dr. G.S. Gujral	Centre for Rural Development and Appropriate Technology Indian Institute of Technology Delhi-110016.
Prof. Iqbal Khan	Department of Civil Engineering Jamia Millia Islamia New Delhi-110025.
Ms. Majida Iqbal	Research Scholar University of Roorkee Roorkee (U.P.),
Dr. Haribabu	Department of Humanities and Social Sciences, IIT Kanpur.
Prof. Lila Krishnan	Department of Humanities and Social Sciences

	Indian Institute of Technology Kanpur (U.P.).
Dr. Shushil	Centre for Management Studies Indian Institute of Technology Delhi-110016.
Dr. V Upadhyay	Department of Humanities and Social Scienees Indian Institute of Technology Delhi-110025.
Dr. S. Karunesh	Centre for Management Studies Indian Institute of Technology Delhi-110016.
Dr. Anuradha Sharana	Department of Humanities and and Social Sciences Indian Institute of Teehnology Delhi-110016.

Contents

Part II : Micro Perspective

Part I
Macro Perspective

1 Social Responsibility of Scientists, Technologists and Managements

S. Sampath*

There are numerous strands in the fabric of science. Some of these originate from purely philosophical and abstract thinking. But the main thrust of science is to attempt to solve problems not previously solved or solve the old problems in newer ways. Any country, rich or poor, has to have a national commitment to the policy of building up, on its own soil, a broad base of scientific endeavour covering the basic as well as applied R & D areas. It is of crucial importance that each country affords opportunities to its truly creative scientists to grow and function in the way their genius dictates. There cannot be two sets of standards in scientific research—one for the rich countries and yet another for the poor countries. Doubtless there will be quantitative differences between them with regard to funding and productivity ; but qualitatively they have to be of the same class. And to be able to provide support to those engaged in extending the frontiers of knowledge,

* Director, Recruitment and Selection at Defence Research Directorate, New Delhi.

each country should put to work team of innovators—the applied scientists whose main concern will be to contribute to the growth of the GNP.

With the exception of a few truly backward regions of the world, all the countries are 20th century technological societies. On the technological highway, they have all travelled beyond the point of no return. Just a few decades ago, even the most astute of visionaries could not guess the pace at which technology would advance. What is baffling is that there is such a serious imbalance today in the global picture of development. In many areas, technology is imbedded in a primitive and stifling social matrix. Yet we cannot arrest the forward movement and stay put. Kenneth Boulding, the eminent economist makes this refreshing point :

> The spectacular changes that have taken place in a small segment of the earth's activity, such as in computer technology or cybernation, should not blind us to the fact that, over a larger section of human society, the great and intractable problem of today is not how to deal with technology that is advancing too rapidly but how to advance it rapidly enough to meet the challenge of fulfilling felt needs.

Science and Technology have the power to obliterate, scarcity and to create abundance ; conquer disease and assure for man a better life expectancy and health care during his journey on earth ; and provide numerous devices that can help to eliminate the pain of human labour and leave time for leisure and the enjoyment of the good things of life.

But these expectations have not come to fruition. Poverty and hunger were never a graver threat than today to large sections of the human population. Life continues to be a mixture of strife and antagonistic urges. Swedish Scientist, Hannes Alfven describes the current dilemma in these words :

> Medical Science has successfully fought epidemics, but has forgotten that the population explosion which has resulted from this success is a serious threat in the long run. Electronics has made communication all the World over even much easier but communication between the rich and the poor in Society is today worse than at any time before. Despite the availability of very sophisticated observational techniques, scientists are unable to observe and understand social condi-

> tions prevailing just outside the walls of their laboratories. In this so-called age of Science, the number of illiterates is increasing at a fast rate. Science pays little heed to what was and still continues to be its primary task which is to fight ignorance, prejudice, superstition and violence wherever they appear. In many respects, the relationship between Science and Society must change. This calls for new thinking and several bold initiatives.

The role of Science in War was relatively small prior to Second World War. The destruction wrought during that War in several parts of the World and the menacing, destructive posture of many nations in the decades that have followed—owing to the power that Science puts in their armouries—have tarnished the image of Science in the public mind.

Besides the horrendous weapons of annihilation, there are numerous ills that afflict human society and these are due to changes brought about by Science and Technology. Some of these applications were conceived of with very good intentions but, in the long term, their consequences have become untoward. Well-known examples are : resources depletion and environmental degradation. Every now and then, a technological innovation starts a new hazard *e.g.* use of DDT ; distortions produced by thalidomide ; climatological changes resulting from altering the characteristics of the atmosphere or the ocean ; experiments in recombinant DNA-technology which may inadvertently produce new plant, animal or human pathogens that may disrupt crucial biological equilibria.

It is possible to conceive of the scientific community itself exercising a policy of restraint and conforming to a code of moral conduct, remembering the plea made by Einstein, for the attention of his fellow-scientists, that the concern for man and his destiny ought to remain the chief motivating force behind all technical effort. Independence of opinion on the part of all concerned, an openness in discussion and a coupling of scientific capabilities with moral values are among the major ingredients of a possible solution.

There is observable a marked imbalance between the rate at which the frontiers of knowledge are expanding and the rate at which the newly acquired knowledge becomes integrated and gets consolidated. The process of integration, making

Science more coherent and hence more easily comprehensible, is a more difficult process than merely expanding the territories of knowledge. Science appears to show no concern for this aspect. In its cold and objective march forward, it has ignored and left behind humanism as a factor in the affairs of mankind.

In our context, a strong-willed movement to integrate Science with Humanities should become the corner-stone of our educational effort. We should endeavour to create a perception in the minds of all concerned that Science supports and clarifies the philosophies of Nature and of man embodied in the arts of the classical cultures.

We should equally strive hard to salvage human values inherent in the cultural traditions of the East and the West and to find in them meaning and relevance for our times. Where Science can help is to accept humanism as its foundation and then lend its methods of observation and reasoning to regions of human experience which lie in the domain of the moral and the ethical and which have thus far evaded an objective approach. It is only within the framework of precise, objective knowledge that we may hope to re-establish the old set of values as a factor of consequence in human relations. This process has to start with the individual, with the introduction of harmony between his inner and outer life, leading to harmony between him and groups and between groups and groups and eventually between nations and nations. The methods of Science can help to demonstrate the validity and force of some truths : that neither truth nor the implementation of an idea is the monopoly of the individual, a group or a nation ; the imperative of co-operation rules out the idea of domination of one group by another ; and progress can take place only on the basis of equality, mutual respect and concern for the common good.

We need to generate a new quality of Science based on the understanding that Science should not confine itself to the pursuit of knowledge for its own sake but should become suffused with a moral force. We have landed ourselves in difficulties because Scientists, with rare exceptions, have been content to be the brick-layers of the edifice of Science. In the

new World that we envision, in order to survive and to progress, the Scientist can no longer practice, as well. In the midst of our pragmatic concerns, we should do all that we can to safeguard this vision of Science and the pursuit of creativity that it inspires.

II

A plea is often made that we should turn away from the complexities of today and go back to the age of simplicity of our forefathers. This means calling a halt to the advance of technology. While it is desirable that we look for simplicity in our lives and evolve value-systems that make the minimum demands on energy, non-renewable resources and environmental conditions, it is quite clear that, in order to meet the essential requirements of food, shelter and clothing of the population, we need to make full and judicious use of all the scientific advances that are taking place ; and many new and innovative developments are called for.

There is a basic dichotomy between the technology that affluent societies practice and the technology that poor is capital—intensive and takes from the bowels of the earth recources that have taken aeons of time to materialize ; is complex and requires specially trained operational ; and is highly centralized in setup and working and is thus more prone to accident and sabotage. Such technology is un-satisfactory from the viewpoint of developing countries because it offers no continuity with the traditional forms of knowledge and human skills that these countries possess and in the repetitive, monotonous systems that have to be set up to further it, there are no meaningful tasks to be performed by the abundant manpower available with them. These countries now have the challenging task of organizing alternate technologies—not low-grade technologies but forms of technology that will look at all the scientific knowledge in the world, not in a derivative or slavishly imitative fashion but in novel and hitherto untried ways. Interesting work lies ahead in several significant areas covering the basic human needs : the seeking of alternative forms of technology for generating or tapping energy ; housing and related amenities ; decentralized

and easily workable sewage-disposal systems ; production of protein from algae ; simple and sage means of contraceptives etc.

Technology presents us with many choices, many of them inter-related, making the task of selection quite complex. Choices are conditioned by values. We identify the values of Society or of an individual by the choices that are made. Values differ and they determine the choices. They change with time. Questions arise, for instance, as to which is more important ; clean air or low-cost fuel ? Are we prepared to change our food-habits in order that others may not starve ?

In a review of the progress of Science, over the last two centuries, one notices the very powerful influence exerted on scientific development by the challenges of specific economic problems in industry, agriculture and transport. As the attitude to these problems was a reflection of the type and level of development of the countries where the advances took place, a certain disequilibrium was inescapable. Consequently distortions occurred not only within the realm of Science and Technology but also in the process of the diffusion of the benefits.

Countries of the West became affluent because they were able to complete their industrial revolution before the awakening of any real political consciousness amongst their industrial workers or the public as a whole. Several of them had the labour and the wealth of colonies at their disposal. They had the wherewithal to meet the demands as and when these arose. Our task has become far more difficult for we started with a political revolution which released long-suppressed aspirations. Demands grew even as we were struggling to establish industry and the means to fulfil the demands. Regional and sectional disparities became aggravated in the process. It is easier for a closed, regimented system to contain demands as well as disparities but this will be at the cost of various freedoms of the individual and even of considerable physical hardship. Very few developing countries have been successful in producing enough to overcome the scarcities of essential commodities. The reasons are not *far*

to seek. The very fact of comparative under-development implies the non-availability of technological instruments, managerial capacities and physical inputs needed for higher production of food and other basic consumer goods. Self-reliant development calls for an increase in national savings ; and this implies the postponement of present consumption for the sake of future benefits.

Speaking to an audience in one of our educational campuses, our late Prime Minister Smt. Indira Gandhi had said :

> My heart leaps up when a new achievement comes to light. How can it be otherwise when one thinks of the power of the human mind, which is so tiny a part of this vast Universe? But, basically, our concern must be with the impact of Science and Technology on the human condition and more especially their bearing on problems of social well-being in our own country.

For years I have been urging our planners and our scientists and technologists to pay greater attention to small problems which affect people's day-to-day living ; to develop methods of using local materials and power-resources ; to utilize intermediate technology to improve the traditional grind-stone or the wheel of the bullockcart, to cite only two examples.

Technology is essential to keep us abreast of other nations and to increase and improve our production but it is no less important to use it for the welfare of the people. There is no conflict between intermediate technology and modernization. On the contrary, it helps to make rural people science-minded and encourage them to participate enthusiastically in the process of development.

If technological societies feel alienated, it is because they have cut off their tangible links with the past and have lost their sense of harmony with Nature. The wisdom of our decisions and the quality of our action will be determined by our character and the nature of our being. The more educated and more highly trained we become, the greater the responsibility on us to work for the social good and to strive for higher values.

Smt. Gandhi concluded her Address with these words :

It is time to give a new direction to Science and Technology—to change the course that has been followed since the Industrial Revolution. We must aim at a unified view of global—not only national—needs. A multi-national effort is needed to solve the elementary problems of all the peoples of the World—in the areas of food, medicine and health-care, housing and education. Research is needed to increase agricultural production with a minimum of inputs dependent on oil and coal. We must prevent the misapplication and the waste of the wealth of our rivers and lakes, forests and mines. We must befriend the sun, the wind and the tides and find ways to utilize some of their tremendous reserves of power for human welfare. A whole new technology of conservation is indicated and a new psychology that will teach people to overcome the logic of the jungle that the stronger has the right to consume more.

III

Technology makes spectacular advances through the use of the scientific method. Concurrently great scientific achievements take place because of the technological tools that become available. We witness development in the interconnected areas of nuclear science and technology, covering nuclear weapons-systems, nuclear power systems, the application of isotopes in medicine *etc*. Nuclear technology has been strongly influenced by scientific advances in materials science, chemistry, electronics and instrumentation. To cite another example, the rapid developments that have come about in the field of Laser Technology have given a new momentum to areas of Science such as Spectroscopy that were areas of fundamental importance in earlier times and were characterized by great discoveries. The new field of Quantum Electronics has emerged from this interplay of advances.

Technology is not limited to the fulfilment of industrial goals and objectives. It has begun to permeate all areas of production and end-use. Examples of such areas are: agricultural technology; medical technology, and, deriving input and strength from scientific discoveries in the field of life-sciences, the new range of bio-technologies.

We must also add Information Technology to this stock of new technologies. It is here to make a powerful impact on the very nature of human society. Aristotle stated that the size

of a political unit is determined by the range of a single man's voice. He was a citizen of the Greek World where all residents of the City-State could be assembled at one place to transact their common business. The entire World to-day is a single community. There is no part of it which is not within the range of a single man's voice ; and, in the present television age, within the reach of a charismatic personality using modern community techniques to manipulate emotions and control reasoning. In today's conditions, the use of television, ushering in the tendency to replace language with imagery, with the latter uninhibited by national frontiers thanks to the advent of satellite-based communication, tends to create a highly impressionistic involvement in global affairs. Besides crossing the horizontal barriers of nationality, the newly emerging communication capabilities assail the vertical stratification of Society. Information reaching out to remote regions on a scale not feasible before creates new aspirations and puts into people's minds desires for new demands. Communication media now break through the traditional fragmentation of Society and reveal outmoded limitations emphasizing that human rights and social aspirations and new knowledge and information can no longer remain the monopoly of rich nations nor of the privileged section in a poor country.

Thanks to rapid advances in the field of Computer Science and Technology, both in terms of hardware and software, the Electronic Computer is proving itself to be more than just a productivity engine. A U.N. Document refers to it as "the intellect-amplifier" invented by man. It is well on its way to becoming a responsive personal companion to ordinary people, at home as well as their work-places. Advances in micro-electronics make information-systems both affordable and sophisticated enough for wide-spread use. The innovation-challenge in this field is not just technical. It lies in the matching of the broad spectrum of new technologies for service to the informational, educational and cultural needs of people constituting contemporary Society.

It is quite obvious that Technology has a key-role to play in determining the character and vitality of the socio-economic system as a whole. Less than a decade ao, the cost of

energy remained a small part of the total cost of any output. This resulted from the historical situation in which the population was small and energy resources in the form of wood, coal, oil and hydro-electricity appeared to be of infinite capacity. Technological development was based on the idea that energy would be available easily and at low cost. Neither of these assumptions is valid today. The world population has escalated tremendously and there is no sign of abatement. It is now clear that the future of human society lies in the development of technologies that are not energy-intensive. This is a distinct change that has come about in a short spell of time. This represents an opportunity for countries like ours to leapfrog into technologies of the future which must be low energy-intensive and where everyone in the World is roughly at the same starting point.

The environment has assumed a position of crucial significance within the last decade or so. Earlier the sea around us, the rivers and the atmosphere were capable of absorbing all the end-products of human activity. It did not matter what waste-products were produced ; and they, when produced, could be discharged into the air, the rivers and the sea. Today the situation is vastly different, with a large and growing population in many parts of the World, increasing human activities and the limited capacity of the earth to absorb the effluents. The environmental protection calls for urgent attention : regulations relating to air and water pollution ; control of toxicities in the short-term as well as long-term ; preservation of the global heat-balance ; control of the temperature of water-bodies. It is clear that the development of future technologies must be directed toward attaining a greater degree of harmony with the environment, through the development of processes that result in lesser generation of pollutants and through steps to absorb or destroy pollutants.

Technologies developed in industrial countries have addressed labour-saving techniques in view of the high cost of labour. On the other hand, our need is to provide gainful employment to large sections of our population.

Energy is expensive and not easily accessible ; the safeguarding of our environment has assumed special significance ; the

provision of gainful and satisfying employment to large numbers of men and women has become a key-issue. We have to look at the technological options in the light of the economic and social needs of our Society. We have to devise our own action-oriented programmes. No one from outside can be of genuine assistance to this in this regard.

The pathway to self-reliance is not to set out to rediscover independently what as already been discovered not to invent what has been invented already elsewhere. It signifies the ability to analyze problems and define tasks and objects ; to obtain specific information that is needed from sources that are willing and can provide what is relevant to our needs ; to acquire self-confidence in our ability to develop what needs to be developed ; to start from a base which may be a mix of indigenous and imported knowhow ; and to more into the future on a contemporaneous basis through bold initiatives and new thinking. Self-reliance needs a national commitment and political will that supports it. It encompasses facets such as technology policy, managerial capacities and technical skills. The most critical requirement is a self-reliant science and technology basis :

We should dedicate ourselves to the following objectives :

—the attainment of technological competence, with special reference to certain strategic areas, making the maximum use of indigenous resources ;
—generation of meaningful and satisfying employment to all strata of Society, with emphasis on the employment of women and the weaker social groups ;
—the use of traditional skills and capabilities, making them commercially competitive, and a continual effort to modernize them to make them competitive in the World of today ;
—maximizing development with minimum capital outlay ;
—identification and removal of obsolescence in existing practices, both in terms of equipment and techniques ;
—fuller utilization of existing capacities and enhancement of the quality and reliability of performance and output.

We should reduce our demands on energy particularly from non-renewable sources ; strive for greater harmony with

the environment preserving the ecological balance and improving the quality of the habitat ; and mount crash-programmes to recycle waste-material and achieve fuller utilization of by-products.

It is time to define with clarity the role of academic institutions in the development of technology and in the transfer of know-how to agencies engaged in production-activities.

Universities and other institutions of higher education are invariably idiosyncratic and it is in general impracticable to try simply to transfer successful patterns from one institution to another. While it is myopic and incorrect to dismiss Universities as remote ivory-towers, it is equally a trivialization of the potential of a University to regard it as standing in relationship to Industry as a supplier to a client, producing graduates and research results on order. The kind of relationship that ought to exist between academia and industry is a subtle one in which the University utilizes its autonomy to try to take the longer, strategic view, in a genuine spirit of co-operation in which, in fact, there is a distinct complimentary of roles, as between the two partners. Technology and its development are immensely important intellectual endeavours that demand the very best of human creative skills.

We should enlarge the scope of functioning of Engineering Consultancy Units of which we have many happy examples with successful accomplishments—to facilitate the conversion of ideas and capabilities from laboratory to production centres. In the process of transfer to technology from the donor to the acceptor, it is essential to provide basic information on those aspects that went into the generation of the technology or a particular design. The availability of such information will help to build the spring-board for further development.

We all recognize that sizeable investments are called for at this critical juncture. If appropriate investments are not made on indigenous efforts, money that is available will flow out on import of goods, capital equipment and technology ; and our backwardness will be perpetuated. In a White paper submitted to the Parliament of India on the vistas of our national development in the fields of Nuclear Energy and

Space Technology, Indian Scientist Vikram Sarabhai made this observation :

> Our late arrival on the scene, our initial backwardness and the meagre investments made by us in the past need not be allowed to remain our handicaps but can be converted into our most valuable assets if we now clearly define our priorities, make judicious investments and take firm forward steps with confidence in our ability to manage our affairs competently.

Ever since we became a free nation, we have made a sustained effort to improve the economy of the country, to grow more food, to lessen the pain of hunger and malnutrition, to generate wider employment and to improve living conditions of the people as a whole. We have attempted to restructure our educational system and meet the awesome challenges posed by the immensity of our population. We have addressed ourselves to the imperatives of self-reliant growth of science and technology to fulfil our felt needs.

We have succeeded on a number of fronts that will help to enthuse us in our efforts to reach higher levels of performance. There are glaring failures too that cast a doubt on our ability to rise above our difficulties and move forward on the path of progress. There is in evidence a rising crescendo of fissiparous tendencies challenging the integrity of those who wish to preserve the unity of the country. The daily newspapers are replete with reports that indicate a sliding down in human values, the onset of violence for securing immediate material gains putting narrow, sel-fish ends over the larger interest of the community and a lowering of respect for truth and purity in public life.

Many of our villages remain untouched by the changes taking place elsewhere. Whatever changes take place are the trickle-down effects of changes in towns and cities brought about by the introduction of modern industry and technology. The rural sector quite often acts as a drag on the rest of the economy.

We complain about the slow pace of change. On the other hand, when change takes place rapidly, certain sections of the community tend to appropriate to themselves a larger share of

the benefits than is their due. A sudden access to wealth, has led to several abuses including a penchant for black money, which started with the business community and has now spread to other classes.

Can it be said that our growth has suffered due to lack of resources ? This may have been true in the early years when nearly everything that we needed for development had to be imported—capital, technology and management skills. Today we are not short of capital or technology or mangement skills. What keeps us down is not lack of resourees but the lack of ability to use them intelligently and efficiently. If we do not develop this capacity, we will surely descend into mediocrity and be pre-occupied with trivial activities.

Over aeons of time, we have developed an ethos in which we prefer individual perfection to creative social action. The Indian desire to unite with the infinite is a distinctive characteristic. Our people have the remarkable capacity to keep the inner man intact, whatever happens around him. There is the story of the Sarpanch of an Indian Village who mentioned with pride that his village had collected Rs. 50,000 to build a new temple. Looking at the pathetic state of the open sewers of the village, the visitor asked him : "Will you not first think of building sewers for the village?" A look of consternation and pain came over the face of the Sarpanch—at the lack of appreciation of the system of values. The Sarpanch is the true representative of India—not the one who put the question.

In the process of civilization, the cake of custom is broken and Society is set in dynamic motion along the course of change and progress. There are two Indian characteristics that we may take note of : One is that we do not fight. We absorb what we wish to absorb and reject most influences on us. We have learnt through centuries to fight these influences but we reject them peacefully. In India, reformers have found that when they try to chip at the cake of custom, it is the chisel that cracks rather than the cake ; for example, the cake of the caste-system or the cult of the dowry-system. Introducing Computers into such a society will not by itself modenise the Society. It will noly help to usher in another item of

greed and exploitation. Modernization has to address itself to the motives, the values and conduct of each person in society.

Arnold Toynbee, the eminent historian points out that, growth ceases, a sense of drift and a sense of sin take over. The sense of drift comes from a belief that the whole world is ruled through chance or by Karma ; that no change can or will come and hence the effort is not worth making. We have lived under the thraldom of drift for centuries and must continue to do so. If there is a sense of sin, there is hope because it can serve as a stimulus for change.

Indian civilization refuses to die like the Greek and Roman civilizations. But it resists also regeneration. We need a new impulse to kindle the heart of India and set it on the path of dynamic progress. To lift the nation from the morass of difficulties, from the frame-work of age-old customs and from the web of indecision, will take more than the determination of one individual, however, sincere, wise and enlightened he is. People must become involved in a programme of positive changes and this must begin with their making the changes themselves in their lives.

All around us we see a heightened awareness of the problems being created by advances in Science and Technology, affecting our environment and threatening the future of the human race. Our concerns transcend our abilities to deal with these problems. We do not yet see with sufficient clarity how we may deploy our resources in a constructive manner and do this even as our scientific and technological capabilities get enhanced.

V

We should rise above certain illusions. Science and Technology cannot wish away poverty at one stroke though they can show how this can be optimally done in the long run. Science and Technology cannot by themselves generate employment or counter under-employment but they can be used to develop appropriate-techniques that may be employed and to analyze their cost-effectiveness in attaining the desired goals. How

Science and Technology can be used to meet human expectations is a matter of commitment to social justice.

The exploitation of knowledge for the benefit of mankind is a complex, arduous process. Human societies are more difficult to deal with than we thought at one time. Every intervention in human affairs produces unforeseen complications. In the ultimate analysis, it is only an incisive understanding of the human factors-combined with the new capabilities that flow from advances in Science and Technology that will help to achieve a World of decency, of increasing opportunity for individual development and of social life based on compassion and co-operation. There is only one choice before us and it is the one that calls upon us to move to a higher level of understanding, of sophistication and of sensitivity in our use of Science and Technology and in our service to Society on mankind's behalf.

Science and Technology affect the lives of all of us. Major decisions involving the investments that we make in the areas of Science and Technology should be the responsibility of all of us. These should be essentially public decisions. This, in turn, demands that all members of Society must be educated and made to feel concerned about the nature of the advances in Science and Technology and their impact on Society. We need the visualization and articulation of a series of humane goals to meet. It is only when we hold this that we will be able to lift Science & Technology from out of the rut into which they have fallen and invest them with meaning and purpose in human terms. We have met here to achieve a discernment of such goals and ways of moving towards them in a manner that is commensurate with our aspirations conditioned by our limitations and constraints.

In the words of Prof. Alfred North Whitehead:

> The future of humanity is filled with threats, hazards and uncertainties. And it is among the merits of Science that it shows us the path towards progress and the way out of difficulties.

This Workshop is an attempt to promote thinking on the *modus operandi*, in our context, of using the advances in Science and Technology to promote the welfare of the Society to which we belong.

2 The Humanistic and Scientific Values in the Pursuit of Seiences*

J.N. Kapur**

Late Dr. G.P. Chatterjee was not only a great scientist and engineer, but was also a great humanist and a great believer in 'Spiritualization of Science' and what he called 'The Science of Human Ethics'. He also pleaded for the fusion of scientific and humanistic cultures and for simultaneous research in the atom and the *atman*. In an address on 'Atom and Man' in 1968 he stated :

> Never before in the history of mankind did man possess such potential source of power from the atom—an atom that could; on the one hand, usher in peace and plenty on this planet and eventually lead man to his ultimate destiny 'Divinity' or 'the divine life', and on the other hand, lead him to discord, destruction and eventual death in a dreadful and dreary radio-active wasteland...Man's future depends on how far the physics of his intangible spirit triumphs over the physics of his tangible body, how far mind triumphs over matter, how far man triumphs over atom.

* Based on the Eighth G.P. Chatterjee Award Lecture delivered at the 75th Session of the Indian Science Congress (1988) at Pune.

** Emeritus Professor, University Grants Commission, New Delhi.

If man has to triumph over atom, the most essential condition is that he must remain a man. He must not give up, at any cost, those spiritual, ethical, moral, social, humanistic, cultural and scientific values which characterize him as man. He can succeed in his goal of divinty if he relentlessly pursues, with all the strength at his command, all the human values which he has inherited. Any compromise or weakness on the front of human and scientific values may ultimately lead to the triumph of atom over man.

Taking my clue from Dr. Chatterjee, I will like to express my anguish at the slow erosion of basic humanistic and scientific values in Science Education and Research in our country. Unless this erosion process is stopped immediately and unethical and unscientific values are banished thousands of miles away from the domain of science, both the spirit of science and the soul of man are likely to wither away.

The goal of divinity of man suggested by Dr. Chatterjee can still be realised if we put our 'scientific house' in order. As Dr. Paintal has said, we have no time to lose. I am sure the scientists who have the courage to send satellites into orbit, will also have the courage to accept the challenge of re-establishing scientific values, in all their purity, in both Science Education and Research.

Some Basic Theses of the Present Paper

—Every scientist has to be a true humanist and a great lover of mankind. He should have a great vision for mankind, in which there will be no poverty, no hunger, no disease of the mind or body, no suffering, no greed, no hatred, no violence ; in which there will be universal love and fellow feeling and in which everybody will be continuously learning from womb to tomb and will be enjoying the learning. His love for science should also be the result of his love for humanity.

—Every scientist shall also be a true scientist. He should imbibe all values for science like originality, creativity, innovation, impartiality, fairness, integrity, objectivity, excitment and passion for new knowledge, love for truth and so on, not only for his scientific pursuits but for all his actions.

—If a scientist tries to follow these values in the scientific work but is otherwise superstitious, unfair, dishonest in his other actions, this lack of integrity in other actions will sooner or later, affect the integrity of his scientific work. A scientist has to be ruthless in his observance of basic ethical scientific values, in case he wants to remain a true scientist.

—In scientific research, the ends are very noble and the means should be equally noble and pure.

—There is a pollution of corruption, nepotism and favouritism all round us. A scientist should not succumb to it, but he should fight this evil with all his might. The first step is that he should observe all the basic ethical and scientific values scrupulously in all his scientific work. The second step is that he should see that all the values are observed with no exception, in the management of scientific institutions. Hopefully, this step will help in removing pollution in the atmosphere outside scientific laboratories also.

—If Science grows tremendously, but the scientific spirit decays and the scientific values decline, all will not be well for mankind and all will not be well even with science, since scientific values are even more important than science itself.

—A scientist should defend scientific values and his own selfless passion, devotion and dedication to science, with all the strength at his command.

—Scientific research is becoming Big Business and just like any other Big Business, it tends to be exploited by self-seeking individuals for whom Science is not a Search after Truth, but is only a means of getting unfair advantage over others. A scientist should see that the Big Business of Science is conducted according to the highest possible ethical standards.

—There are thousands of dedicated scientists in our country and in the world, but there are also a few pseudo-scientists who want to exploit the Science System for their narrow personal ends, their designs have to be foiled in the beginning by an enlightened public opinion.

Value-Oriented Science Education and Research

The erosion of human values in our educational institutions has been a matter of great concern. A number of our educational thinkers have expressed their grert concern about it.

Two National Symposia have been held to discuss ways and means to restore human values in our educational system.

There is a similar erosion of scientific values in our scientific research. The Society for Scientific Values is doing excellent work in creating a public opinion against the unethical practices in scientific research.

All the crusades launched by dedicated individuals and groups deserve all the support both in speech and action.

We discuss some of the unethical practices which are causing tremendous damage to Science Education and Research in our country.

Erosion of Scientific Values in Science Teaching

Some unscientific values are transmitted to the students in school science laboratories themselves. They are encouraged to results. Students are asked to verify some scientific results with imperfect instruments and then are encouraged to get perfect agreements with theory by manipulating the observations. Teachers themselves declare : "What does it matter if a few observations are changed to get good agreement ?" They do not realise that through this practice, they are teaching foregory, they are teaching something against which science has always fought. They may be teaching some facts of science, but they are killing the Spirit of Science.

Students sometimes do not perform experiments themselves, but copy the results from others' practical note books. Sometimes teachers themselves encourage students to do so, so that the authorities may get the impression that all the students have done all the experiments. This happens usually when the equipment is not sufficient for all the students to perform experiments.

It is not uncommon that in many schools and colleges, equipment for performance of only 40 to 50 per cent of the experiments prescribed by the Board of University is available. The teacher requests the examiner to examine th e students out of only those experiments and the examiner is given a party at the expense of the examinees. Many examiners of practical lessons are approached by parents, teachers and otherwise decent citizens to do favours to some students. One wonders

whether in this way we are 'educating' or 'miseducating' our students in science.

Even the learning of science is not through the discovery process, but by committing some facts to memory, without understanding all the implications of those facts.

To crown all this is the final murder of the scientific spirit when mass copying takes place in *public science* examinations.

It is important that the government should see that every science school and college is equipped with all the necessary equipments for all the experiments prescribed by the examining body, that the school managements and teachers see to it that the students perform all the experiments themselves before they appear in the examination, that the 'cooking' of results is regarded as a scientific crime which should be looked down upon by every student and teacher and science examinations are conducted so as to discourage cramming and copying.

One of the basic aims of teaching Science is to teach the Scientific Spirit, the Scientific Methods of Enquiry and the Process of Science. These are even more important than the facts of science. Every lesson in Science should emphasize these basic values of science.

Ultimately it is only a strong public opinion of teachers, students and parents which can restore scientific values of science.

Erosion of Scientific Values in Scientific Research

Manipulation of results of scientific experiments to make them fit certain theories is not an uncommon practice in research. I realised this some years ago when as a vice-chanellor, I was present in one Ph D. viva-voice examination of a Zoology candidate. He showed some slides of eggs some of which were apparently lying in heaps. When I asked him how he had counted those eggs, he said casually, "I ignored all of them." In this way, he claimed that he had disproved an earlier theory. What was surprising was that his supervisor supported him by asking immediately. "If he could not count them, what else could he do ?" This illustrates the non-scientific value of taking the easy convenient path rather than the correct path which may be difficult.

If found a similar case in a medical thesis, when the candidate came to me to get my help in the statistical analysis of his data. I was surprised to find that all his entries were in terms of even numbers. When questioned, he told me that he was to undertake one hundred case studies, but he could get only fifty patients. His supervisor therefore advised him to multiply all the entries by two. This type of manipulation is quite common in some social science theses, depending on results of surveys, in cases where very few people reply to questionnaires sent by investigators.

Many persons become Ph. Ds in science by following completely unscientific procedures.

Another unscientific or unethical practice is noticed in the names of authors of research papers where many persons who have nothing to do with the actual research in the paper are shown as authors. In some laboratories, the name of the head of the laboratory and the name of the head of a group occurs in every paper sent from that group though these persons may not know even the A B C of the papers. The claiming of authorship of papers which one has not written is completely unscientific and unethical, but sometimes this practice leads to some such persons being dubbed as great scientists and their winning prestigious national awards.

Another such similar unethical practice arises because some universities insist on an internal supervisor being associated with a supervisor external to the university system. The external supervisor does all the guidance, but the internal supervisor who knows nothing about the thesis also gets the credit. Some persons become professors on the basis of the fake research guidance experience and even examine theses in the subjects in which they have provided this fake guidance.

Other unethical practices include (i) publishing of unrefered papers by charging "page-charges" (ii) appointment of 'convenient Ph. D. examiners' (iii) examination of Ph. D. theses by persons not working in the fields concerned (iv) yielding to political and other pressures in Faculty appointments.

It appears that many persons engage in scientific research not for the sake of love of Science or love of truth or the

excitement that scientific research alone can give, but for the sake of undue advantages received. This explains the sharp decline of research productivity of a person after getting a Ph. D. degree or after becoming a professor.

Science as Big Business

Some years ago my daughter got an offer of a fellowship from a Professor in Canada for research in physiology. To see his credentials, I went to the medical college library, went through Medical Science Abstracts and was happy to find that the professor was writing, on an average, twentyfive papers per year in good journals. As such I gave my daughter permission togo and work under his guidance. After a year I went to Canada and I was invited by him to a dinner. I naturally congratulated him on his research output. He hesitated for a moment and then confessed, "Most of the papers you saw were not written by me. I got grants of a few million dollars every year from the government, I gave followships to bright students, I buy costly equipments and I let the students work on problems considered important by the government funding agencies. They write research papers, write my name on these papers so that I may get more grants and they may have no financial problems. I go to the laboratory only when new equipment is to be installed. This was not always the situation. Eight years ago, I used to spend sixteen hours a day in the laboratory and I was doing first-rate research, but I found that the credit for those papers was going to my boss who was always the first author. I then decided to become a science manager and I succeeded. I sometimes have a guilty conscience and I feel I was happier when I was an active scientist".

This is the story all the world over. When Science in India was on a small scale, most of the scientists worked in their laboratories. Now that science in India has become a large scale affair, many of them have become managers of big science, control large funds and have praises and prizes showered on them. The Mathews effect becomes operative *viz* "More power will be given to those who have large powers and from those who have small powers, these will also be taken away."

Mighty governments place large funds at the disposal of the big science managers and ask them to achieve results consistent with their aims in peace and war. These managers then give contracts to smaller managers who are their friends and whom they know and trust. The pure scientist who does not want to spend time in getting and managing funds, works in his laboratory with relatively smaller resources. In fact every scientist has to spend some percentage of his time in getting funds and his percentage may vary from five per cent to ninety per cent.

Science as an Industry

Whether one likes it or not, Big Science is a reality today. Scientific knowledge is sought to be manufactured in the same way in which other more-tangible products are manufactured. There is a public sector and there is a private sector. There is a large scale science industry and there is a small scale science industry. The small scale industry sometimes acts as auxiliary to large scale science industry. Fortunately there is still some place for individuals with bright ideas, but they are also being encouraged to group together.

Science as a Profession

In scientific industry human beings play a major role and machines have still not become dominant. However, the role of sophisticated scientific equipments, computers and robotics is increasing and the role of the individual scientist is decreasing. Science is, however, still a profession and peer recognition is still a major motivation for scientific research. There are, however, signs already that a politically powerful scientist may receive more honours than a scientifically powerful scientist and if this trend continues, science as a profession may decline. Moreover, group efforts and team efforts are becoming more important than individual efforts and in this case recognition is also given to groups and teams. The groups are, however, identified by the names of their leaders and the leaders may be those persons who get funds for the group rather than those who really do the work.

Science and Religion

Sometimes man worships science in the same spirit in which he worships gods and goddesses. He builds large temples for science, instals costly equipment there and prays for results. He is even tolerant of irreligious practices in temples and of unscientific practices in science laboratories. However, unless the priests in a temple are deeply religious and unless the devotees go there for worship of deity and not for asking for undue advantages over others, no progress in true religion takes place. Similarly unless the scientists in a laboratory are truly dedicated to science and are not interested only in getting undue advantages over others by cornering costly equipment, no progress in science can take place.

Progress of Science and Character of Man

The following question is raised again and again : "Why is it that with meagre resources earlier, we were doing relatively well in science, but with much larger resources now, we are not doing so well and why our scientific ouput is not commensurate with the input of funds and the number of scientists ?" I am discussing this question because it is ultimately related to the subject of Science and Man on which I was asked to speak.

The number of scientists has increased many many times, but the number of dedicated scientists has increased much less. This implies that the number of non-dedicated scientists has increased much faster than the number of dedicated scientists. Scientific output depends on the number of dedicated scientists. In fact the non-dedicated scientists have a negative effect on the quality of scientific output.

It has been suggested that this is because we compromise with mediocrity, but why do we compromise with mediocrity ? This happens because we compromise with vested interests, we yield to pressures, social or political and we are prepared to oblige those who oblige us in other ways. We compromise because our dedication to Science and Society is much less than our dedication to our friends. Men who are committed to the highest humanistic and scientific values will never compromise with mediocrity.

It has also been suggested that we, the senior scientists, should encourage the younger scientists. This is unexceptionable, but how do we define senior scientists ? Are these those persons who have been continuously thrilled and excited by research over long periods of time, who are still active on the frontiers of knowledge and who still spend 10 to 14 hours per day in their laboratories. If so, they encourage young scientists, by their examples. They have not to say a word to the young scientists, yet these young scientists will be inspired to put on their best.

If on the other hand senior scientists are those who have attained senior status by virtue of age, who are no longer active in research, who control vast resources because of their positions and who are generous enough to part with a fraction of these resources for the young research workers to encourage them, this encouragement will not be fruitful.

The only way we, the senior scientists, can encourage the young scientists is being hundred per cent active in research, by breathing science, and living science, by being examples of fairness, objectivity and dedication but not compromising with mediocrity under any conditions, by ruthlessly insisting on merit in promotions and by using all funds at our disposal for promoting science and national interests and never for promoting, even unconsciously, our own personal interests.

Only upright men can produce upright scientists. If we have to develop Science in India, we have to have men of steel, ruthless in their pursuit of Science and Truth.

The other side of the coin is even more important. The young scientists should also take upon themselves the responsibility of encouraging senior scientists, by doing first rate science, in spite of all the handicaps and difficulties and by their dedication to Science. Let them have high ambitions and goals. The achievement of every young bright dedicated scientist gives encouragement to all senior scientists. It fills them with hope for the future of Science in India. Let the young scientists learn only from the examples of the most dedicated senior scientists in the country. Fortunately we have still a large number of shining examples for young scientists to follow.

How is Science doing ?

Science is doing extremely well. For the last hundred years, it has been growing exponentially with a doubling period of about ten years. This means that if we had one unit in science in 1900, we had two units in 1910, 4 units in 1920, 8 in 1930... 256 units in 1980 and we shall have 512 units in 1990 and more than 1000 units in the year 2000.

This means that in the year 2000, we shall have about 1000 times as much science as we had at the beginning of the century. This also means that 99.9 per cent of the science we have today has been created in this century and that 99 per cent of the scientists who ever lived have lived in this century. This also means that in order to keep up-to-date with the explosion of knowledge a scientist has to work very hard indeed.

The exponential growth follows from the mathematical model : rate of growth of science at any time,

$$= k \text{ (amount of science at that time)}$$

The constant k depends on the investment of funds and the dedication of the scientists. If developing countries have to catch up with the developed countries they have to increase their investments and dedication of their scientists significantly, otherwise the gaps between developing and developed countries are going to increase.

The doubling period applies to all factors *viz* the number of Ph. Ds, books, research papers, journals, funds spent, number of scientists and so on. For the number of scientists, the doubling period cannot go on indefinitely because the doubling period of the human population may be 25 years or so and if the doubling period of scientists is ten years or so, it is easy to see that one day there will be more scientists than human beings. This can happen only if we have robot scientists and machines with intelligence as good or better than that of human beings. This might as well come out to be true !

The Impact of Computers and Informatics on the Pace of Scientific Discovery

The availability of knowledge-based simulation techniques, electronic laboratories, electronic libraries, vast knowledge-

bases stored in computers, decision-support systems, computers capable of proving theorems and discovering patterns in complex situations. Computer-controlled manufacturing systems, robots *etc.* will vastly accelerate the pace of learning and research. As Dr. Raj Reddy said in his recent convocation address at IIT, Bombay, "Computers and Communications can truly revolutionise the nature of research and education in the twenty-first century. Each one of us can have a personalised intelleetual assistant which could use voice and vision for man-machine communication, tolerate errors and ambiguities in human interaction with machines, provide education and entertainment on a personalised basis, provide expert advice on a day-to-day basis, make vast amounts of knowledge available in an active form and make ordinary mortals capable of superhuman tasks, leading to new discoveries and inventions at an unheard of rates".

Science and Man

I was asked to speak on some aspects of Science and Man. On the one hand a great scientific future beckons mankind. Science may grow a thousand fold in the twenty-first century. Every one will have a chance to attain great intellectual heights. The brilliance of a thousand Suns of Knowledge will be available to us.

On the other hand, the Scientific Spirit characterised by objectivity, rationality, integrity, impartiality, fairness, tolerance, excellence and truth seem to be declining in science itself. Unless we reverse this trend and pursue Education and Research in science in the true Spirit of Science, Growth in Science will not mean Growth in Wisdom and Character and the net result may be that man may be much further away from divinity than he is to-day, if man survives at all during the next century.

As such we should be rulthless in insisting on scientific values in all Education and Research and in all walks of life. These values are ultimately the same as the great humanistic values. Without these values man is doomed ; with these values, he has a great future.

The growth of Science is going to change the relation between Science and Man. The nature of this change will depend on our values and our wisdom.

Let each one of us do some soul-searching, and do only those actions which are worthy of the great values of science and none others.

3 | Going Beyond the Intellect : A Gandhian Approach to Scientific Education

T.S. Ananthu*

It is said that when Mahatma Gandhi was asked, 'What do you think of Western civilization', he replied, 'I think it would be a good idea'. This concise answer to such a major question carried with it, simultaneously, a great deal of humour as well as provocation for very serious contemplation. At that time, however, it was ignored because everyone took it for granted that 'progress' of the kind being made in the West represented the highest ideals of civilization, something which the less affluent (and hence less civilized) should be striving for. It is only now that a few intellectuals—just a few, really—are beginning to wake up to the shortcomings of 'progress' as currently defined, and so this is an appropriate time to take a fresh look at the foundations on which our concept of progress has been based.

Two mighty pillars on which Western civilization (and this includes those of us in the East who have become modernized) rests are modern science and modern education. Over the last century or so, science has gradually come to occupy

* Gandhi Peace Foundation, New Delhi.

the pride of place in the education system, and even non-science subjects have been given a scientific orientation and modern education have supported and reinforced each other through what may be termed 'scientific education'.

In recent times, there has been a growing feeling that something is wrong somewhere with our education apparatus, and many suggestions (and a few reforms) have resulted. In this research document, however, the aim will be to suggest changes not in the system of education, or in the structure through which it is imparted, or even with regard to its beneficiaries, but in *the contents of the education process itself.*

The contents of the education process in western civilization, as well as in all modern schools and universities the world over, have been exclusively 'outward—oriented' : gathering knowledge about the world around us, and analyzing that knowledge using our intellect. There is nothing wrong, as such, with 'outward-oriented' education. In fact, the tremendous progress that we have made on the material front is a direct result of such education. But it is time for us to realize that outward-oriented education by itself is not enough, and that we cannot overcome the severe tests and crises mankind is facing today unless and until we supplement this with 'inward-oriented' education aimed at transforming the inner core of the student, making him* more compassionate, more considerate, more altruistic.

Are there techniques, or education processes, which can make a man more compassionate, considerate and altruistic ? Even though largely unknown to the educated elite of today, such processes and techniques *do exist*. There processes operate unlike modern education, at levels beyond our intellect, and deal with our inner being, the core of our existence. With their help, any man or woman could transform himself or herself in truly wonderful ways. The potential offered by these processes is beyond our wildest dreams. With proper training and dediction, one could even rise to the heights of a Gandhi or a

* Throughout this paper, the use of the words 'him' and 'man' as referring to humans has been made for the sake of convenience, and should not be confused with any form of chauvinism.

Buddha—who knows, may be even higher. The methods adopted by the teachers of such processes are highly scientific. Just as modern science conducts studies in and experiments with what is outside of us—minerals and metals, oceans and hills, suns and stars, electrons and protons *etc.*—similarly these teachers* teach us to study and experiment with what is inside of us—*e.g.*, our reactions to events, our attitude towards others, *etc.* Just as modern science aims at teaching us to become 'lord and master of nature' (as Descartes put it) by means of these studies and experiments, similarly these processes aim at making us master of our own nature, *i.e.*, our own self.

How come the modern world is largely unaware of these processes ? These reasons can be traced to the emergence of

---

* The term 'mystics' has often been used to designate such teachers, which is itself indicative of our neglect of this subject. We have shrouded all inward—directed education in a mystery, hence the term 'mystics' to refer to those who are adepts at it. The term 'enlightened seer', or 'saint', conveys the meaning slightly better.

Of course, there are genuine mystics as well as fake mystics or quacks. In Section III, reference will be made to a simple test for distinguishing between the two. It is the fake ones, and those who have commercialized these sacred traditions, who generally obtain a lot of publicity and attention.

In this connection, it is worth noting what Robert Ornstein, the famous psychologist at the University of California Medical Centre, has to say : "As a Psychologist who studies consciousness, I try to separate the inflated metaphysics, the goofiness, the outright lies and the commercial reductionism from the real possibility of Eastern disciplines". After a detailed and scientific study, he concludes "These Eastern modes of knowledge complement orderly rational inquiry. Our ignorance of them has left a fundamental gap in our approach to reality, leaving us with a one-sided, hyper-rational view of the world." In the course of this inquiry, Ornstein discovers the real reason why fake teachers of mysticism manage to draw followers : "Our own lack of technology for developing consciousness has left a seedy, unknown area that has spawned charlatans, fast-buck operators and instant self-improvement teachers who come and go."

In other words, quacks thrive because we have refused to study this subject scientifically. As the Sufi mystic Jalaludin Rumi, whom Ornstein quotes approvingly, had said : 'counterfeiters exist only because there is real gold'.

modern science and modern education as dominant systems which originated in the context of the rebellion against religious persecution, dogmatism and obscurantism. This trend, however, did not confine itself to the removal of the ills of institutionalized religion, but, because of the exclusive stress on the intellect that developed, proceeded to discard and deny the very essence of religion, thus *throwing away the baby along with the bathwater*. We have rightly discarded the superstitions and dogmas that plagued us in the name of religion, but while doing so we have adopted a completely materialistic world-view and value framework, thus turning a blind eye to the existence of those wonderful processes which enable us to strive towards the High. The result is that our educational institutions teach us everything—how to become an engineer, a doctor, a statistician, a librarian, a programmer, a technician *etc.—but not the most important thing* : *how to become a better* (*i.e. more humane*) *human being*. Thus, the major problem that existed during the pre-scientific days continues to haunt us even now. As the highly perceptive journal '*Manas*' has observed.

The age of religion and the age of science—however much their claims and rationalizations were in conflict - had one great consequence in common : both led to the politics of power. The modern world is now in the throes of a great debacle—the failure of power . . . . In very nearly all directions, increasing applications of power are proving counterproductive.

But science *has* given us one advantage, one wonderful faculty. Over the last four hundred years, it has taught us to question ourselves, to probe deeper and deeper, and this attitude can generate a "searching of our souls" which could prove to be our redemption. As '*Manas*' has observed in another recent issue :

The best thing about science—which may prove its saving grace—is that it can be turned against itself. An institution which does not shut out self-correction is a remarkable achievement, not often duplicated in historical experience.

Indeed, 20th century science has led to discoveries which point to a direction diametrically opposite to the one that

Western civilization has come to represent. As the physicist Fritjof Capra has observed :

> Most of today's physicists do not seem to realize the philosophical, cultural and spiritual implications of their theories. Many of them actively support a society which is still based on the mechanistic, fragmented world-view without seeing that science points beyond such a view, towards a oneness of the universe which includes not only our natural environment but also our fellow human beings. I believe that the world-view implied by modern physics is inconsistent with our present society, which does not reflect the harmonious interrelations we observe in nature. To achieve such a state of dynamic balance, a radically different social and economic structure will be needed : a cultural revolution in the true sense of the word. The survival of our whole civilization may depend on whether we can bring about such a change. It will depend, ultimately, on our ability to adopt some of the 'yin' attitudes of Eastern mysticism ; to experience the wholeness of nature and the art of living with it in harmony.

Scientists like Capra are realizing the tremendous significance of Gandhi's statement about the inadequacy of modern civilization, and are working towards what Vinoba once termed 'the confluence of science and spirituality'. In the following sections, we will see how scientific education can be re-moulded to reflect this confluence and thus enables us to take the next jump towards a more civilized, a 'post-industrial', society.

II

OBJECTIVITY AND RATIONALITY : EXPANDING OUR HORIZONS

Modern science prides itself, and rightly so, on the concepts of Objectivity and Rationality which form the essence of its foundations. Objectivity demands that what one man can others observe, can observe too : *i.e.*, the observation must be independent of the observer and hence repeatable by one and by all. Rationality requires that what is to be deduced, derived or explained must be done so in logical (reductionist' or analytical)

terms. Scientists do not confer the term 'scientific' to any observation unless and until it has passed the test of objectivity. Similarly, no derivation or conclusion gets the appellation 'scientific' until it has passed the test of rationality.

The 'scientific method', as presently practised, normally consists of four distinct stops—(i) asking the question (generally arrived at by means of observation and/or analysis (ii) postulating a hypothesis (iii) conducting one or more experiments and (iv) arriving at a 'law' or generalization. The third step is based entirely on the principle of objectivity and so, to a certain extent, is the first. The fourth step is only if it is derived from the principle of valid rationality, which also generally plays an important role in the first. The second step, hypothesis formation, is the only one in which "intuitive" or "non-rational" modes have sometimes been reserted to, though very rarely. But even in such cases, the ultimate acceptance or rejection of the hypothesis has always rested on its validation by the objective and/or rational modes.

The twin principles of objectivity and rationality* have been so eminently successful in the physical sciences that they have gradually been extended into what used to be known as the 'humanities'. In economics, in sociology, in psychology, in political science and other such subjects, the 'scientific method' borrowed from the physical sciences has been introduced. For example, the famous social scientist Vilfredo Pareto described his approach in the following terms :

The field in which we move is therefore the field of experience and observation strictly. We use those terms in the meanings they have in the natural sciences such as astronomy, chemistry, physiology, and so on, and not to mean those other things which it is fashion to designate by the terms 'inner' or 'Christian' experience . . . if (political economy and sociology) would progress, it is imperative that they should follow the example set by the physical sciences.

In the last few decades we have seen a great deal of progress

* As will be shown later, there is an intimate relationship between these principles. The two are complementary to each other, and should not be viewed in isolation.

along the lines that Pareto desired. Mathematics and statistics have been introduced into sociology, and psychology linear programming and matrix theory into economics, sophisticated intricacies into political science, and computers and systems analysis into anything and everything. But has all this made our treatment of the humanities truly scientific ? In order to get an answer to this question, let us apply the test of objectivity as developed by the scientists themselves.

We know that when two physical scientists watch an experiment in a laboratory, they are essentially in agreement about what they see and how they report the observation : this is what makes the principle of objectivity work. But what about in the social sciences ? For example, in November 1979, when the much publicized 'event' of the capture of 52 Americans in Teheran took place, how was this event observed ? Local social scientists gleefully reported the 'arrest of 52 spies as a just retribution for decades of interference and exploitation', and many outsiders—especially in the Soviet Union—tended to agree. But, of course, many other social scientists, especially Americans, viewed the same event as 'an illegal detention of 52 innocents in flagrant violation of all international laws'. Similarly, an 'observation' of the state of affairs in, say, Kazakistan, would be reported as a 'Russian Empire' by the typical western social scientists and as "the smooth functioning of the Soviet Republic of Kazakistan' by his Russian counterpart, with the Iranian this time siding with his American, not Russian, colleague. So, despite all the mathematic and the sophistry, the ideal of 'objective knowledge', unaffected by the sway of human emotion and above the blandishments of wishful thinking, continues to evade the social scientists.

The situation on the rationality front is similar. When two physical scientists, whatever their background, are presented with data from a set of observations, they generally reach the same or similar conclusions, which is what gives life to the principle of rationality. But when two social scientist are deeply influenced by their background. For example, in whatever form we may tabulate the world's poverty statistics, a Marxist social scientist will interpret the underlying cause to be exploitation of the working class by the capitalist class,

the capitalist social scientist will analyze it to show that shackles or controls on free enterprise is what is causing the problem, and the Fundamentalist Islamic social scientist will probably trace it to our lack of faith in Allah : each, of course, regarding himself as perfectly rational and the other as totally irrational,

How did this situation come about ? Why hasn't the effort to make the humanities truly scientific succeeded ? To get an insight into this vital question, let us recall the warning of Robert Oppenheimer :

> . . . the worst of all possible misunderstandings would occur if psychology should be influenced to model itself after a physics which is not there anymore, which has been quite outdated.

Oppenheimer was referring to the difference between 19th century and 20th century physics. Nineteenth century physics, based on the Cartesian-Newtonian-Darwinian world-view, dealt with those aspects of the world which may be termed gross or visible, *i.e.*, phenomena accessible to the ordinary senses : stones, pendulums, chemicals, minerals, *etc.* Twentieth century physics, by contrast, has investigated deeply into the realm of the highly subtle or the deeply invisible : sub-atomic particles on the one hand, and astronomical speeds on the other. As many physicists such as Bohn, Capra, Davies *et. al.* has been at pains to point out, the world-view of twentieth century physics is completely at odds with that of 19th century physics.

Surprisingly and unfortunately, however, the commonly accepted 'scientific world-view' continues to be based on 19th century physics. The result has been that the ideals and definitions adopted by social scientists have been based on 19th century models of science. The error involved in this is not merely one of obsolescence, but has much, much deeper implications. *The definitions and concepts accepted in 19th century science, especially those relating to objectivity and rationality, pertained to the gross or visible, not to the subtle or invisible.* As modern physics has shown, these definitions completely break down in relation to the very subtle and the

highly invisible : and, in subjects that deal with human beings, such as psychology or economics or sociology, it is the subtle and the invisible that is of the greatest importance. The subtle and the invisible side of man—his hopes, his desires, his fears, his doubts, his speculations, his ambitions, his likes and dislikes, his thoughts, his idiosyncracies, his mind and, above all, his consciousness—is undoubtedly of far greater consequence than his gross or visible side. The truly vital aspects of man are far more subtle than even the hadrons, pions or photons that physicists deal with. Hence, by adopting methods and processes of 19th century science, social scientists have ignored the really important aspects of man and have, in a sense, treated him akin to stones or pendulums. This is the fundamental cause of the failure of scientific techniques in the social sciences.

How can we rectify this error ? An essential first step is, obviously, to re-define our concept and scope of objectivity and rationality so as to make them applicable to the subtle, not just to the gross. In this endeavour, we can profitably make use of the efforts of 20th century physics. But we must not forget that the key lies in grasping the essence—the philosophy, the vision—of quantum and relativity theories, and not just the mathematics involved. In fact, confining ourselves to the latter amounts to sticking to the gross and refusing to see the subtle*.

Let us start by taking a look at how quantum and relativity theories have transcended the ordinary concepts of rationality. Most concepts in these two realms of physics would seem irrational to the extreme from the ordinary common-sense

* A good example is the concept of 'waves' that is used to describe sub-atomic particles. Unless we imbibe the essence from a conceptual point of view, there is a danger of regarding the 'waves' referred to as akin to water waves or sound waves, which is entirely wrong. In reality, it can actually be compared to the 'Indira wave or 'Janata wave' that we have witnessed in India's general elections : in both the sub-atomic worlds and the election picture, the 'wave' represents not an actual entity which can be seen physically, but a highly abstract 'probability pattern' whose effects get manifested. This, incidentally, illustrates how concepts developed in 20th century physics can be made use of by social scientists.

point of view. Paul Davies has termed them "so shattering to be almost beyond belief—even to the scientific revolutionaries themselves" and has traced their 'stranger than fiction' nature to be the reason why "their full implications are often not appreciated, even by many professional scientists".

The seemingly irrational nature of the answers provided by quantum physics comes through clearly in the words of Oppenheimer :

> If we ask, for instance, whether the position of the electron remains the same, we must say 'no' : if we ask whether the electron's position changes with time, who must say 'no' ; if we ask whether the electron is at rest, we must say 'no' ; if we ask whether it is in motion, we must say 'no'.

Until the advent of quantum physics, statements such as the above would have definitely been classified as 'irrational'. Even now, in any scientific investigation of the gross or visible aspects of reality, such a statement would still be termed irrational and hence unscientific. But in the highly subtle realms, when dealing with sub-atomic particles, the situation undergoes a dramatic change, and seemingly irrational statements are regarded as highly scientific.

What has happened, in essence, is that we have recognized that our intellect in its common form has a severe limitation : it can deal only with the gross and the comparatively less subtle aspects of the reality around us. It cannot comprehend the more subtle aspects of reality. Hence, without expressly saying so, scientists have made an important modification to our concept of rationality. Instead of dividing conclusions into the rational/irrational categories, *we now have three compartments in which to place them* : irrational, rational, and supra-rational.* Of these, only irrational is unscientific. Both rational and supra-rational are scientific, the latter even more so than the former.

Relativity theory also abounds in 'supra-rationality'. There is, for example, the famous twin brother paradox : if one of two twin brothers were to travel into space at a speed significant

* I am indebted to Dr. D.S. Kothari for this terminology and this way of viewing the results of quantum theory.

when compared to that of light, on his return he would be significantly younger to his brother. The imaginary possibility* of someone who can break the barrier imposed by the speed of light is also worth mentioning because of the hilarious limerick it has given rise to :

There was a young lady named Bright.
Who could travel faster than light
She went out one day
In a, sort of, relative way
And came back the previous night.

We thus reach the conclusion that in dealing with the very subtle, what is highly scientific would nevertheless be seemingly irrational at the gross (or even less subtle) level. So, in order to deal with the full range of the subtle (including the subtler aspects of human beings), we must recognise *levels* of rationality.

---

* As the effort to deal with human consciousness from a scientific point of view gathers momentum, crossing the barrier imposed by the speed of light may not be regarded as such an imaginary possibility after all. Even now, we know that while it take light eight minutes to traverse the distance from the earth to the sun, our mind can 'go' there in a split second. We may argue that mind is not a 'thing', but then what is a 'thing' ? As we go deeper into the real nature of everything around us, our efforts to arrive at 'the' fundamental building blocks of matter are giving way to the rather startling conclusion that, in the ultimate analysis, there is no such thing as a 'thing'. Once this gets accepted, it would not take us long to realize that the 'solid' aspects of matter we see around us, and the highly abstract aspects of life such as thoughts, desires, *etc.*, can all be represented on the same spectrum, the distinguishing factor being one of subtlety or invisibility.

Arthur Young's masterstroke of genius in classifying the photon not as a sub-atomic but as 'action analogous to human decision', and in viewing the universe as an arena where such action (rather than 'things' or matter) is basic portends the kind of development that could completely change our materialistic concept of the reality around us. Every scientific revolution erupts by solving the mystery hidden in what an earlier paradigm considered 'a constant', and unravelling the mystery behind that constant 'c' used to designate the speed of light could herald a truly major scientific revolution.

Before we discuss the implications of such a modification to our concept of rationality, let us see how the other foundation of modern science—objectivity— can also be modified to cater to the full range of the subtler aspects or reality. We know that modern physics, especially in dealing with sub-atomic particles, has put aside the classical requirement of objectively : that the observation must be totally independent of the observer. This requirement was set aside because, at the very subtle level of sub-atomic particles, observation is possible only by interaction. The result is that the very act of observation alters the system, so that no experiment is repeatable in the classical sense of the term. An extreme example of this is the case of the photon, whose very observation results in its annihilation. In practice, of course, this can never happen, because a photon (or, for that matter, any sub-atomic particle) can never be isolated, but this example does illustrate dramatically how different the world of the very subtle is from that of the gross.

In order to arrive at a concept of objectivity that would be applicable to both the gross and the subtle, let us take a deeper look at our present definition of objectivity : the correct, true and full form of reality is that which is discovered by means of observations and experiments independent of the observer, *i.e.*, anyone can perform it and will see and report exactly the same thing. There are, however, two hidden assumptions in this definiton. One (and a rather trivial one) is that blind persons are excluded from the 'anyone' category, for they cannot obviously see and report the same. The other, and more interesting one, is this : we are assuming that a person with good or perfect eyes can see everything that there is to see. In other words, we are assuming that the visibility range of 0 per cent to 10 per cent is fully represented by the physical condition of the eye.

Is this assumption correct ? To get an answer to this question, let us recapitulate how the eye functions : by responding to electromagnetic radiation that impinges on it. Reproduced on the next page is the electromagnetic spectrum range as currently known to science. At one extreme are cosmic rays, with frequencies around 10^{28} cycles/sec., and at the other end

TABLE I
The Electromagnetic Spectrum Range

(Figures appearing in this diagram are taken from Fritjof Capra's *The Tao of Physics*.)

Frequency in cycles per second	*Types of wave*
10^{28}	
10^{26}	Cosmic rays
10^{24}	
10^{22}	
10^{20}	Gamma rays
10^{18}	
10^{16}	X-rays
Visible light	light waves
10^{12}	
10^{10}	radar
10^{8}	FM radio waves
10^{6}	TV AM

Our eyes respond to only a tiny fraction of the above spectrum, sandwiched in the 10^{14} to 10^{15} cycles/sec. region. Even if all frequencies below and upto 10^{15} became visible to the eye, this works out to only 0.0000000001% of 10^{28}, upto which the spectrum is definitely known to extend. Of course, one could argue that the occurrence of waves is not uniformly distributed over all frequences, and that the correct calculation procedure should take into account this distribution. But do we really know the actual occurrence of waves in the 'invisible' regions ? Are we not continually discovering new and totally unexpected phenomena in these realms ? In any case, however, the calculation is performed, there is no doubt that our eyes respond to only a small fraction of the total radiation around us.

are amplitude modulated radio waves, at frequencies around 10^6 cycles/sec. Of this, visible light occupies only a tiny, tiny part ; sandwiched in the 10^{14} to 10^{15} cycles/sec. range. Percentagewise, this works out to less than 0.00000000001% of the total frequency range. And this takes into account only that part of the electromagnetic spectrum already known to science : who knows how much smaller it might work out when more is known ?

So, our concept of objectivity needs to be modified to take into account an extremely important but neglected fact ; all observations performed by human beings operating at ordinary levels of consciousness take in only a minutesimal portion of reality. This portion represents the 'gross' part. The 'subtle' part, which is also by far the larger, gets filtered.

This does not mean that we get to know nothing about the subtler aspects of reality. We certainly do, as is evidenced by our knowledge of the electromagnetic spectrum way beyond the visible range. But such knowledge is acquired by indirect perception, not direct perception : *i.e.*, by applying our faculty of reason (or intellect) on information gathered by direct perception. In fields of knowledge where direct perception will do—such as distinguishing a colour or recognizing a friend—there is no need for the intellect : it could in fact act as a positive barrier. But when information is not available by direct perception, indirect perception is the only way : thus, for example, we *deduce* the existence of cosmic rays by witnessing (an act of direct perception) the patterns created in the bubble chamber during a 'cosmic shower'.

This leads us to the complementary nature of the principles of objectivity and rationality. The grosser part of the reality around us can be observed by our ordinary senses (or consciousness) using direct perception, and the principle of objectivity is needed to ensure its scientific content. But the subtler aspects of the same reality have to be deduced using our intellect, *i.e.*, by indirect perception, and the scientific nature of such a deduction determined by the principle of rationality. Thus, indirect perception or the principle of rationalty is required only because direct perception or the

principle of objectivity does not tell us everything : in fact, it tells us very, very little.

But deducing is obviously not as foolproof a way of knowing as seeing. When we see a colour or recognize a friend, we know for sure that we have done so : no amount of argument can shake our belief. By contrast, when we use our intellect and reach certain conclusions, our beliefs are 'unshakable' only as long as the theories on which the deductions have been made remain intact. At the less subtle levels, they seem unshakable because the theories are based on observations at the grosser level, which were obtained by direct perception. But as the level of subtlety increases, the dependability of rational conclusions decreases—as evidenced by our frequent revisions of theories underlying such phenomena. And, finally, a stage is reached—as has been shown by relativity and quantum theories—where the degree of subtlety is so far removed from our capacity for direct perception that reality seems to be in direct conflict with rationality.

Hence, we have to recognize a basic difference between scientific knowledge obtained by direct perception and that by indirect perception. The former may be considered objective, but not the latter. Because the term subjective has an unscientific connotation, let us term scientific conclusions arrived at on the basis of the principle of rationalty as 'projective' ; this indicates that the knowledge has been obtained neither by directly seeing the object concerned, nor by wild or personal guesses, but by projecting the image of the object on to the surface of our mind, which is the best that can be done in the absence of direct perception.

To summarize, then, we can say that scientific knowledge can be obtained in the following ways :

(i) By using the principle of objectivity, in realms where direct perception is possible. Most human beings have their physical senses intact, which allows direct perception of the grosser part of reality, But this is only a minutesimal fraction of the total.

(ii) By using the principle of rationality, in realms where no direct perception is possible. This results in 'projective' knowledge, which is quite accurate in the less subtle realms but grows hazy and/or unreliable as

the level of subtlety increases, until finally in areas like subatomic phenomena or space-time intraction it has to be abandoned altogether in favour of what may be termed 'supra-rationality.'

In scientific education as understood at present, the stress is exclusively on the development of analytical skills—*i.e.*, on increasing our capacity for indirect perception. It has been assumed that our direct perception capabilities are given and fixed. But there has existed all through human history, in all ages, in all lands, in all traditions a small group of teachers (sometimes just a handful) who have insisted that this assumption is wrong. Examples of such teachers who lived in the past but are well-known at present are Kabir, Nanak, Christ, Buddha, Shamz-i-Tabriz and Maulana Rum.* They could be referred to as 'mystics' or 'enlightened seers' or 'saints'. What is important is not the way we address them, but their teachings : and they have all taught that given adequate preparation and effort, any human being can increase his or her level of direct perception and, obviously, as the coverage of direct perception increases, so does the range or clarity of indirect perception.

Unlike modern education, which aims at sharpening the intellect, the mystics or enlightened seers teach us to transcend the intellect and attain levels of 'supra-rationality'. Their teachings, could, therefore, be termed 'education beyond the intellect'.

III

EDUCATION BEYOND THE INTELLECT

In essence, education beyond the intellect involves raising the level of functioning of our consciousness. What is conseiousness, and how does raising its level result in enhancing our capacity for direct perception ? To understand this, let us take a deeper look into what is involved in direct perception.

Direct perception takes place through our senses—sight,

* Though they may not be well-known, such teachers exist today too. Education beyond the intellect, by its very definition, can never be learnt by books alone, and hence requires living adepts or teachers.

hearing, small, taste and touch. Each of these is associated with a physical organ—*e.g.*, sight with eyes. We normally assume that we see because of our eyes. In a sense, this is of course correct, because if we are deprived of the eyes we are also derived of our sight. But this way of looking at the situation blinds us to an extremely important aspect of our ability to see—that is, that our eyes act only as instruments in the process called seeing. This becomes obvious if we contemplate on what happens at death. As we know, for a short while after death, the eyes remain intact, which is what enables 'cornea grafting' operations to take place. So, what shuts off sight at death is not the loss of the physical eyes, but something else, which we may term as 'consciousness'.

Thus, it is not the eyes which see. It is our consciousness using the eyes as an instruments which does the seeing. Therefore, sight is not only as function of the condition of our physical eyes, but is also dependent on the state our consciousness. An analogy of a nail being driven with a hammer could be useful here. As we know, without the hammer as an instrument, we cannot drive the nail in, but the hammer would be powerless to do so by itself—it needs a certain power behind it, and its ability is very much dependent on the nature of this power. If the power is a mechanical device, the hammer may function most efficiently, but only in a limited way. If the power as a human being, the hammer can be put to use in a variety of ways depending on the intelligence of the human being. If the human being has the subtle touch of a sculptor, an incredibly fine piece of art can result. Similarly, the 'sight' revealed through the eyes depends on the power of the consciousness that is using the eyes. A mechanical mind would see less than an intelligent mind. And a mind that functions at a subtler level of consciousness would make use of the eyes in ways that would seem incredible, unbelievable or impossible at the grosser level of functioning.

The importance of the role of our state of consciousness in determining what we see becomes clearer if we reflect upon the true meaning of that famous saying : 'beauty is in the eye of the beholder'. The same piece of painting may be regarded as very beautiful by a connoisseur of art and as 'just a mixture of

colours' by the ordinary person. What accounts for the difference ? It is the consciousness of the beholder. At the gross level, they both see the same—a piece of canvas with colours all around. But the connoisseur, unlike the ordinary person, has adequate 'sight' (in the form of the level of consciousness that operates the eyes) to perceive the subtle too—and hence is able to see the beauty that exists. Similarly, an adequate level of 'hearing' is required to appreciate Bade Gulam Ali Khan or Beethoven : so it is not the ears, but the consciousness that is behind it, which is the primary factor behind what we hear.

Beauty and music are two areas in which 'direct perception' capabilities of a particular kind are required. It is worth noting that neither of the two is comprehensible merely by analysis : both have to be grasped 'as a whole'. Another such example is poetry : as Wordsworth put it, 'it is murder to dissect poetry'. Yet another field where 'holistic' understanding is required in everyday life is in the grasping of a joke. A sudden 'illumination' has to take place as soon as the punchline is uttered : having to explain the punchline is equivalent to rendering it sterile, to killing the joke.

The differences in the ability of human being to appreciate beauty or music, understand poetry and grasp humour indicate to us that, just as people are born with different capacities for analysis or indirect perception, there are also small differences in our capacities for direct perception. But, as we saw in the last section, the ordinary human being's capacity for direct perception is extremely limited : not even one billionth of the total potential. What mystics teach us is that our consciousness, and hence this direct perception capacity, can be increased unbelievably, to areas undreamt of. So, when they speak of 'third eye', or '*drishti sadhan*' or '*tisra til*', they are not referring to anything physical, but to the state of consciousness of the person. Thus, when the Buddha was asked what accounted for his enlightenment, he simply said, 'I am awake'. indicating thereby that (i) our sight is accounted for by "consciousness operating on the physical eyes" rather than just the eyes and (ii) in the non-enlightened state we are all,

in a sense, asleep—unaware of all but a billionth part of the reality around us—because of the low level of our consciousness.

At this stage, it is necessary to put down a note of caution. As we know, whatever is accessible to us direct perception is also manipulated by us in fairly easy ways. We also know that the subtler aspects of reality contain much more power than the grosser aspect : as our knowledge of electricity laser beams, gamma rays *etc*. has revealed to us. So, if a person develops direct access to the subtler aspects of reality in much the same way as we have to knives and hammers, he would also have access to the unique powers inherent in these subtler realms. What we must never forget is that any misuse or display of such power (what our ancients called *riddhis* or *siddhis*) goes contrary to the basic aim of the education being imparted. What is this basic aim ? In terms of what we studied in Section II, we can look upon the basic aim as increase in the level of objectivity. Objectivity, as opposed to subjectivity, involves getting rid of the 'self,' and here is where any missue or display of *riddhis* or *siddhis* violates the very purpose of 'education beyond the intellect'.

Hence, a truly good teacher of mysticism concentrates exclusively on ridding his student of the 'self' within him. He exhorts his students to not even be aware of the powers that accrue in the process. As the Chinese Master Lao Tsu put it to his students, 'not to know that one knows is best'. Rather than involve their students in powers that give a boost to their self-importance, mystics aim at just the opposite : increasing the field and degree of objectivity by reducing the 'self'. As the Buddha put it in simple yet unambiguous terms : 'There is self and there is Truth. Where Truth is, self is not. Where self appears, Truth is not'.

Reducing the 'self', or becoming truly selfless, is the same as increasing love, for after all love is nothing but 'losing one self' ; we lose ourselves in the object of our love. *So the correct process of enhancing direct perception by increasing our level of consciousness involves the development of love or selflessness to the exclusion of everything else.* But the standards by which 'the enlightened' measure love are extremely rigorous.

For example, Christ exhorted us to 'love thy neighbour as thyself'. This may seem like routine moralizing, but it is much more than that. There is a big jump involved in graduating from 'loving thy neighbour' to 'loving thy neighbour *as thyself*'. The latter is possible only if we can identify ourselves totally and completely with our neighbour ; if he feels hungry, we must feel an equivalent amount of hunger : if he feels pain, we must feel an equivalent amount of pain. Such identification is not possible as long as we regard the neighbour's body and ego as different from our body and ego. Under normal human consciousness, our mind finds it impossible to dissociate itself from our own body and our own ego : and it is here that 'education beyond the intellect' comes to our rescue. It develops a Christ—like love within us by breaking our association with our body and our ego. The entire training that teachers of direct perception enhancement impart is centred around this. Exercises like meditation that they prescribe are meant to train our mind to rise above the normal confines of the 'self' or ego. As Dr. E.F. Schumacher has described it :

The Christian is told 'to love his neighbour as himself'. What does this mean ? When a person loves himself there is nothing standing between the giver and the receiver of that love. But when he loves his neighbour his own little *ego* tends to stand in between. To love one's neighbour as one loves oneself, therefore, means to love without any interference from one's own ego ; it means the attainment of perfect altruism, the elimination of all traces of egoism . . . (Through proper inner development education) one day we may get to the point when we can do this so perfecty that *we*, little "egos" with their own needs, perplexities, and difficulties, do not come into this picture at all. Such total absence of *ego* would mean total objectivity and total effectiveness.

The development of perfect altruism as described above is definitely a challenging task, involving attention to the smallest of trifles in our day-to-day activities and functioning : including a constant watch on those self-centred, egoistic thoughts that coast through our minds, mostly without our realizing them. Such meticulous attention to itrifles may seem like too much

fuss about un-important things but then, as Michelangelo put it beautifully, 'Trifles make perfection, and perfection is no trifle', and so any striving towards 'perfect objectivity' necessarily involves being constantly on the guard against the 'self' creeping into our activities and our thoughts.

The rewards of such an education are also in proportion to the super-human effort involved. As we become increasingly and perfectly self-less in our thoughts and actions, superhuman consciousness sets in bringing along with it enhanced direct perception, thus taking the student literally from the ordinary *Atma* level to *Mahatma* levels and towards the *Paramatma*. As Christ put it, the idea is to become like God. "Be ye perfect, as your Father is in heaven." And he insisted that each one of us has the latent potential to make the jump to super-human levels : "Ye are gods and all of you are children of the most high." Kabir said the same thing in different words, indicating by two similes the unbelievably fantastic transformation that each one of us is capable of, and also warning us that the task is a challenging one :

जैसे तिल में तेल है, चकमक में आग ।
तेरा प्रियतम तुझ में, जाग सके तो जाग ।।

We can thus see that 'education beyond the intellect' follows a path entirely different from education of the intellectual variety that we are used to. The results, are entirely different. Modern education results in improving our rational abilities, but not our scope of objective vision, and thus keeps us away from direct knowledge of the supra-rational regions. Education beyond the intellect, by contrast, increases our level of objectivity so as to include not only the gross but also the subtle, thereby increasing our knowledge capability by leaps and bounds. But the principal objective of 'education beyond the intellect' lies in an altogether different share : transforming us into infinitely better (*i.e.*, more humane) human beings, and thereby enabling us to stick to our principles in the face of the gravest temptations and challenges. It is by means of such a transformation that our material progress can be towards making our lives meaningful and happy, and making society civilized even by Gandhi's standards.

Education of the intellect and beyond it are by no means exclusive, and can very well be taken to simultaneously by anyone. But it is important to bear in mind, as we studied in detail in the last section, that education at the purely intellectual level gives us only a hazy notion of what lies in the subtler realms, and hence shuts us off from true and objective knowledge of these aspects. As Kabir made it clear, the subtler aspects of reality can never be grasped by means of the intellect alone, but need the development of heroic levels of selflessness or love :

पोथी पढ़ि-पढ़ि जग मुआ, पंडित हुआ न कोय ।
ढाई अक्षर प्रेम का, पढे सो पंडित होय ।।

It is obvious that Kabir is referring to a *pandit* very different from the kind we are used to. He is referring to one who has, by dint of selfless love, opened his vision to the subtler aspects of the universe surrounding us. Once the subtle vision opened, the world that we live in will be seen in a very different, and much truer, light. Investigations in physics have already confirmed, by means of knowledge obtained through indirect perception in our laboratories, how the universe when viewed with knowledge of the subtle seems strange and unbelievable compared to the universe without such knowledge.

The implications of the findings of modern physics has already spurred several great thinkers to suggest that these could be of great help in our daily lives and in a study of the humanities or the social sciences. As our eminent scientist-cum-educationist Dr. D.S. Kothari has observed about the 'complimentary' principle that is central to an understanding of sub-atomic physics :

The idea of complimentarity has deep philosophical and epistemological implications. Niels Bohr earnestly hoped that one day the complimentarity principle would be a part of school and general education for everyone . . . Its moral is tolerance and harmony through deeper understanding. An understanding and sense of complimentarity would afford the guidance and strength we need in life.

Bohr himself had imbibed this principle so well in his personal life that J.A. Wheeler spoke of him thus: "Bohr's own

deep understanding of human problems, and his powerful influence over those around him, make one certain that men like Jesus, LaoTse, Confucius and the Buddha really lived." This goes to show that what is called for is not so much an understanding of the mathematics involved in the complimentarity principle and other ideas of modern physics, but the personal transformation that results by *imbibing* the ideas : something that can take place only by a mental transformation of the kind mystics speak of. Not that there is anything wrong with learning the mathematics involved : but the imbibing will take place only when one forces the mind to learn to operate at a level 'beyond the opposites' and into the realm Christ spoke of when he asked us to love others as ourselves. As the Buddha put it : "Learning is a good thing but it availeth not. True wisdom is availeth by practice only. Practice the Truth that the men there is thou." For such a practice, we have to turn to 'education beyond the intellect'.

It is interesting to note that not only Bohr but others such as Heisenberg, Schroedinger, *et al.* to whom we owe the great ideas of 20th century physics displayed saintly qualities. Einstein, who made the greatest contribution, was also the closest to a saint. What is more, he made it very explicit that his scientific insights came not from rational arguments but from enhanced direct perception of the mystic variety : "I do not arrive at any understanding of the fundamental laws of the universe through my rational mind . . . The cosmic religious experience is the stron gest and noblest mainspring of scientific research." So, while experiments of the kind performed during the 1919 eclipse by Eddington have enabled the scientific community to accept the theories of modern physics, the origin of the theories themselves must be traced not to the principle of rationality as currently defined but to the special direct perception capabilities of a select scientists.

It is also worth noting that great and noble souls, even those with no scientific background and no formal 'education beyond the intellect', have clung to world-views that correspond to the 'irrational' variety. Two examples from the present century are Mahatma Gandhi and Mother Teresa.

These statements indicate that great and noble souls are born with direct perception capabilities way above the normal, enabling them to at least 'dimly perceive', as Gandhi put it, the subtler but more important aspects of the universe we live in. This brings us to one great benefit that can result if we incorporate 'education beyond the intellect' into the mainstream of our lives : we could help ordinary humans to rise to the levels of a Gandhi, a Teresa or an Einstein, thus creating hundreds or thousands of them.

Even those who cannot reach the levels of a Gandhi, a Teresa or an Einstein would still end up becoming better and nobler human beings. Hence, the human race as a whole would move towards the creation of a New Man, the ideal of all great revolutionaries and visionaries. This vision was well conveyed by Leon Trotsky who dreamt of the day man would "become immeasurably stronger, wiser and subtler. His body will become more harmonized, his voice more musical. The average human type will rise to the heights of an Aristotle, a Goethe, a Marx." It is enhancement of our direct perception capabilities by means of 'education beyond the intellect', rather than merely a change in the structure of society, that can lead to the fulfilment of this admirable goal.

4 Values and Beliefs vs Growth of Science and Technology

Pankaj Sharan*

Introduction

Material needs of a society determine a social and economic structure. These needs are fulfilled by technological tools and reliable, systematized knowledge called science. If the society has solved the problem of survival—at least for a sizable privileged section of it—there are in addition certain psychological and spiritual needs which for their fulfilment require arts and literature, philosophy and religion.

In order to study the relationship of values and beliefs prevalent in society to scientific and technological activity one must study the collective aspirations and needs of the society in question.

The aim of this paper is not to study relation of values and science in any particular society or epoch in history, although there are a few remarks at the end about present day climate. The paper only makes some general remarks on the symbiotic relationship between values and beliefs on the one hand and science and technology on the other.

* Department of Physics, Jamia Millia Islamia, New Delhi—110025.

Favourable Climate for the Growth of Scienee and Technology

If one looks at those periods in history where there has been very rapid growth of science and technology—like the Greek golden age, the rise of Islamic Science, the renaissance in Europe or the 20th century throughout western world—and if one tries to link it to the prevalent values in society one finds unmistakable symptom. That symptom is what can be called an open attitude to knowledge. It can be summarised as follows :—

(i) Knowledge is considered to be a commodity accessible to all and not the property of a privileged few.

(ii) Addition to the store of knowledge is encouraged.

(iii) Exchange and dissemination of knowledge is done vigorously.

(iv) Conflicting views are hotly debated (not always successfully) instead of being sealed separately in tight compartments.

Of course, there is a precondition for the existence of this attitude. There must be enough leisure available to some sections of society to indulge in search for knowledge. And the existence of such a section, in turn, requires an economy which supports it.

It is not being suggested that such attitude to knowledge is the *cause* of growth of science and technology. Instead developments in technology produce economic climate which encourages such attitude to knowledge. So the relationship is symbiotic in nature.

Impact of Science on Values and Beliefs prevalent in Society

Revolutionary discoverics in science have caused deep and permanent changes in human thinking and beliefs. It is sufficient to just mention the impact of Newtonian mechanics. Darwinian theory of evolution, Relativrity and Cosmology of Einstein, Uncertainty principle and genetic engineering.

Since this question has been studied in great details by historians and philosophers of science, it is sufficient to make just one clarifying remark.

In studying the impact of science and technology on values it is essential to separate the two. It is a widespread view that the interaction of Science and Society takes place via the *interface* of technology. This is wrong. This view is popular due to the visible fact that practical needs of society are fulfilled through technology and development of technology often depends on scientific discoveries. This view seems to ignore the conceptual or spiritual needs of society—the need for a worldview, a comprehensive picture of the universe. True, this need is often overhelmed by the struggle for survival, but is nevertheless there, otherwise how do we explain the existence of religion even in the most primitive stages of society? Science affects this conceptual, mental picture where technology affects the practical day-to-day lives of people. If one can say, technology affect our *external* lives whereas science influences our internal, mental lives.

Role of Individual in Scientific Discovery

Even if the prevalent norms and values in society influence people generally, it is ultimately an individual who makes a discovery. When we discuss the influence of values and beliefs on scientific development we face the following triply difficult problem :—

(i) The influence of prevalent values on a particular individual.

(ii) The influence of these values on a particular discovery.

(iii) The influence of that discovery on development of science. This problem is further complicated by the fact that individuals who contribute to major scientific discoveries are hardly the *typical* members of their social milieu.

Despite these difficulties. commentators, critics and historions of science have tried to find in the birth of a new idea the influence of prevalent values. Some scientists, notably Einstein, have offered important clues to these influences. Briefly:

(i) A belief in mathematical (or more generally rational) comprehensibility of the world is common to all scientists. The belief goes very deep—to an intensity of a religious fervour.

(ii) Aesthetic values such as beauty, simplicity, a desire for a unifying principle play a very significant role in formulation of hypotheses.

(iii) Einstein has emphasized the role of moral qualities like non-conformation, strength of character, perseverance, rebellious attitude to authority *etc.* in making the correct scientific attitude.

Present scientific climate and values

The age of science which dealt with immediate world of experience is over. The scientist now uses very sophisticated and indirect tools to study the very small or too big. The physical sciences are exploring the realm of subatomic particles, or the remotest parts of the universe. It is the biological sciences which are likely to affect our values and beliefs. Our picture of man, his mind and behaviour is strongly influenced by developments in the fields of gene expression and genetic engineering. Eventually, questions of living, non-living and religious concepts like good will also be brought into the realm of scientific enquiry.

It is encouraging to see that the open climate for scientific enquiry has come to stay in most parts of the world. The number of scientific works has also increased phenomenally, especially after Second World War. The rapid influence of scientific knowledge and technology especially on under developed societies has been studied in detail, and there is little that can be said generally.

5 | Some Reflections on the Education of Engineers

V.N. Arora*

During my school days I read a One-Act play called "Monkey's Paw". In this play there is a dried-up monkey's paw whose owner's wish is fulfilled but in such a way that he rules the day who came into possession of that paw. For example, there is an old couple who wish for twenty thousand pounds to buy a house, and a few minutes later an insurance inspector arrives with a cheque for twenty thousand pounds—compensation for the death of their only son who died in an accident in the factory where he worked. Whenever I think of technology as an instrument of socio-economic change, I am reminded of this play.

Let me cite a few examples of what technology has done to us. We have the Indraprastha Thermal Power Plant which partly meets the needs of power of this city but the price we have to pay for this facility is that we have to inhale hundreds of tons of coalash and carbon monoxide and diaoxide that this plant belches out. Delhi provides another excellent example, to solve the problem of transport of the ever-increasing population, the engineers' solution is to put more buses on

* Department of Humanities and Social Sciences, IIT. Delhi.

the roads that were never meant to cope with this density of transport vehicles. And the fumes emitted by some of the buses are to be seen to be believed. No civilized city of the world would permit some of these buses to ply for a single day but the Delhiites feel grateful for this facility. I feel like crying and laughing simultaneously when I think of what the craze for industrialization has done to almost all our rivers, including the Ganga, the holiest of the holy rivers. The irony of introducing automation in country where unemployment figures are mounting every year cannot be lost on any sane man. I think the point has been made that technology is like the monkey's paw because it fulfils our wishes but we rue the day when we set out on this path.

Now-a-days attempts are being made to create an awareness among technologists, engineers and managers about the impact of their technologies and management techniques on social and natural environment. In my opinion it is like putting the cart before the horse because by the time the technologist or the manager occupies a position of power and influence, he is too old to learn. He is more likely to perpetuate the system that has placed him in that position of power and influence. Common sense tells us that it would the suicidal for him to reverse that trend even when he realizes that his system is detrimental to the interests of his society. Altruism is not one of our present-day virtues, anyway.

Values are imbibed by people when they are young and quite often they operate at the subliminal level. Our homes which imparted values to the young have abdicated this responsibility for a variety of reasons, the chief among them being the parents are not sure what values to teach. In the words of a senior colleague, "What values can you teach when all of them are in flux ?"

Schools which reinforced the values learnt by children at home are now commercial establishments. Their goal is "the bitch-goddess success", because in their annual reports principals of schools proudly proclaim how many of their alumni have joined engineering, medical or commerce colleges. I haven't come across a single report in which a school principal has ever mentioned the number of their pupils who have joined social sciences or humanities courses. It is not the

principals who are to blame. The malaise lies deeper ; it is the entire society whose thinking has become vitiated. For this state of affairs our planners, administrators and political and social leaders must accept the responsibility squarely.

The present 10+2 school system stops teaching social studies at the end of the tenth year, especially to the science students. In the liberal arts stream we find only those students who failed to make the grade for the science stream. By and large, the country looks up to the students in the science stream to take her forward. And in their last two years at school, all their energies are channelled into preparing for competitive examinations for admission to engineering and medical colleges. They become victims of the rat race with which we are all so familiar. And once these rats are caught in this maze of success, they are doomed for the rest of their lives. Concentrating on the successful entrants to engineering colleges and ignoring the rest for a while, I see that they continue participating gladly in the rat race of grades and marks. They are taught efficiently how to design efficient machines, and how to run them efficiently. At no stage, or at best very rarely, are they taught how to calculate the cost of their efficient machines to the society that they are supposed to serve. They learn to serve themselves—very efficiently. To expect of them at the fag end of their careers that they would get out of the maze and develop a holistic view is rather too much. Having learnt expertly how to press the right levers getting suitable rewards, how can they be expected to press the levers that would deny them their rewards and could give them electric shocks as well ?

I know I have pointed a dismal picture but is there a way out ? Yes, perhaps, if . . . If I didn't have hope, I wouldn't be wasting my breath and time. Hope is kindled in my heart by the presence of so many of my colleagues here and their earnestness.

I suggest a two-pronged attack on the problem of lack of social awareness among engineers and technologists. The first step is a large number of orientation courses and field trips for teachers in engineering institutions to acquaint them with the mess that our technologies have created. To avoid any

risk of misunderstanding, let me state emphatically that I have no intention of undermining the role of engineers and technologists in raising the standard of living of entire mankind. Perhaps, at no time in human history had the race a higher standard of living than today's. What I sugggest in utter humility is this : let every teacher visualize imaginatively, and if possible empirically, what possible consequences can follow from the specialization he is teaching. The steam engine is not just a steam engine. It initiated certain socio-economic and cultural changes to which the engineer or the engineering teacher paid no heed initially. But now he can't shirk his responsibility. For instance, social awareness of the dangers of research in the area of genetic engineering in the U.S. made these researchers give up this area of research. Do we have any such compunctions or restraints ? I am afraid we haven't even broached the issue as yet.

To achieve this objective, the case studies of the existing technologies will be a useful starting point. How to overcome or eliminate the ill-effects of the technologies being used in the country now will provide meaningful areas acquire a holistic view on the problems of technological research, and may be of life as well. Narrow specialization will not remain the sort of evil that it is portrayed out to be.

The second step is to re-examine the course content of the existing four-year B. Tech. and of the integrated five-year M. Tech. programmes, and make suitable modifications. In my encounters with teachers of engineering subjects what impressed me most were their pre-occupation with and insistence on teaching as many courses in engineering as possible. One cannot help commending their goal to "produce" as well-equipped an engineer as possible. So, in all committee meetings convened to finalize the course content, they claim the lion's share of the students time/credits for teaching engineering course. Unfortunately they forget two things : (a) the rate at which technology is progressing and converting today's frontiers of technologies into backwaters of tomorrow's technologies ; (b) their keenness to convert engineering colleges into super-IIIs (I mean industrial training institutions)

where only training of an advanced type is imparted and education takes a back seat.

Personally speaking, I think a certain amount of obsolescence in education is inevitable but it can be minimized. That engineering colleges attract the best students of the country is common knowledge, therefore, it should be assumed that as intelligent students they can easily pick up information regarding the technical needs of their jobs. As a consequence, the emphasis should be on teaching them where to look for information and how to adapt it to their specific needs. It will not be significant how many courses they have done, so long as they know the fundamental principles and how to apply them in a known or unknown context. What I am implying is this ; engineering teachers and administrators should not insist on asking for the lion's share of the students' time. If they recognized that engineering colleges have also the responsibility of imparting education, which has been sadly neglected at the +2 stage of their schooling, they will be more flexible in their demand for the maximum share of the students' time. As an example, I will cite the case of some engineering departments in IIT Delhi which float courses in the time-table slot meant for Humanities and Social Sciences courses, and make it compulsory for their students to take/opt for those courses. They have reduced the entire system of free floating credits to a mockery. Similarly, some department advisers compel their students to opt for/not to opt for a particular course.

I will make a very broad distinction between "useful" courses and "useless" courses. Useful courses are those courses that belong to the discipline in which a student wants to specialize—say electrical engineering or textile engineering courses. Under this category I would include also those courses which enhance a student's comprehension of efficiency in the area of his specialization. This covers areas like mathematics, computer programming, engineering arts and sciences, *etc.* The so-called "useless" course include all those subjects which don't serve any of the above-mentioned purposes. In other words, they are not utilitarian. Philosophy, Religion, Culture, Literature, Painting, Music, Politics, Psychology, History *etc.* constitute this fuzzy area of "useless"

subjects. In the past, a study of some of these disciplines constituted the education of a gentleman. The necessity of earning one's livelihood may have pushed these disciplines to the back seats in our system of education but it does not mean that we don't need them at all. There is no need to pay them lip service by alloting them a few credits for they teach us aesthetics, logic, ethics, man's place in the universe, rule and justness of law. In short they teach us values—social, moral, aesthetic—which shape our lives. In all courses an attempt should be made to compel our students to make choices and to give reasons for their choices. Though the "useless" courses are more amenable to this approach, it can be used in all courses.

Instead of receiving ready-made solutions, students should be forced to find their own solutions based on values that they have chosen for themselves. It does not matter whether our values are in flux ; once they begin to choose and are aware of the consequences of their choices, they are bound to choose correctly. The emphasis will shift from a pre-occupation with themselves alone to a realization that we live a social context and we share a common fate. Problems can be framed and identified in all disciplines that have more than one solution, and our solution should be superior to the rest depending upon what values or sets of values from the criterion/criteria. The aim should be develop attitudes which will make certain goals more desirable than others. It is the same perental problem of ends and means. Permit me to quote an old prayer :

> Show us not the aim without the way.
> For ends and means on earth are so entangled,
> That changing one, you change the other too ;
> Each different path brings other ends in view.

Our students should be taught to question our goals and having accepted some goals they should be asked to choose means that will not alter the goals. Technology is a means to an end, not a goal in itself. The orientation courses for teachers that I mentioned earlier will come in handy here.

To achieve these goals—a holistic view, training to earn a living and education ; learning how to live—I propose a new division of time and credits. Discipline specialization should

not claim more than 50 per cent of the total time and credits. Every speciality teacher must devote part of the time allotted to him to discussing the pros and cons of various solutions discussed in the class. Atttempts should be made to avoid giving ready-made solutions which lose sight of interdependence of all parts of nature.

Allied and other useful courses should not claim more than 25 per cent of the total time/credits. Emphasis must be laid on the fundamentals and their versatility in use. And the remaining 25 per cent time/credits must be reserved for the education of not only the engineer but the whole man. Let him learn some of the "useless" subjects, depending upon his aptitude. Springs of creativity are drying up, moral values in decay, the degradation of our natural environment is a matter of shame which we all share. How long can we go on neglecting this aspect of the education of our students? And at what cost?

6 On Evolution Socially Responsible Γechnologists

P.L. Dhar* and R.R. Gaur*

Introduction

Though the growth of science and technology has been almost concomitant with the advent of Man, the question of social responsibility of scientists and technologists is a very recent one. More specifically, this suspicion that science and technology can be "socially irresponsible" seems to have arisen only after mankind has become aware in last few decades, of the serious consequences of environmental pollution, ecological damage and nuclear hazards which are direct offshoots of modern technology. This itself suggests that there is something very special with modern technology, which wasn't in the technology of the yore, and which is responsible for the origin of these "social" problems associated with it. A relook at the roots of modern technology is likely to be helpful in locating this special feature.

* Mechanical Engineering Department, IIT, Delhi.

Roots of Modern Industrial Technology

Traditionally, technology has been viewed as systematization of industrial arts which evolved over generation in response to societal needs. Indeed, most of the technologies before the industrial revolution were evolved in direct response to the basic needs of the society for convivial survival *viz.* the needs for food, clothing, shelter, rest and relexation *etc.* Consequently the question of any serious social backlashes never arose, for any technology which could have harmful consequences was never approved. As mentioned by Jacques Ellul, during the high middle—ages when Christian world view reigned supreme in the west, the "technical activity didn't escape Christian moral judgement. The question, "Is it righteous ?" was asked of every attempt to change mode of production of organisation. That something might be useful or profitable to men did not make it right and just. It had to fit a precise conception of justice before God. When an element of technique appeared to be righteous from every point of view, it was adopted, but even then with excessive caution—only inventions judged worthy were applied or even allowed to become known."[1] In fact, the greatest engineer/inventor of all times, Leonardo-da-vinci destroyed some of his drawings of submarines since he felt that "it was too satanic to be placed in the hands of unregenerate men."[2]

The industrial revolution, however, marked a change in this basic motivation. The objective of technology was not fulfilment of the societal needs but, as pointed out almost eighty years ago by Gandhiji[3], maximization of the profit of the producers, often by pampering the baser instincts of man. In the sober words of historian Lewis Mumford[4],—"There was a sharp shift in interest from life values to pecuniary values. The system of interests which only had been latent and which had been restricted in a great measure to the merchant and leisure classes now pervaded every walk of life. It was no longer sufficient for industry to provide for livelihood, it must create an independent fortune." It was this crass materialistic attitude which saw workers only as "tools" to an end and permitted and promoted their unremitting exploitation as revealed by the horror tales of worker's plight in the

mills in England soon after industrial revolution. Consequently, over last two centuries, technology escaped meaningful social evaluation, the only criteria for acceptance or rejection of a technology being, whether it was profitable to the manufacturer or not. It is this fundamental shift in the objective which has resulted in the evolution of a brand of technology—the modern industrial technology—which to quote Barry Commoner[5], "... is admirably suited to the needs of the manufacturer" but ill-suited for true human welfare. The roots of so-called "social-irresponsibility" of modern technologists lie in this "original sin" and therefore the edifice of social responsibility should be built on recognition of this cardinal fact, and a clear understanding of what constitutes integral human welfare.

Technology Assessment and World-View

The type of technology which is evolved and supported by a societv is strongly dependent on the criteria adopted by the society to assess it. These criteria, in turn, depend upon the world-view of the society, its perception of what constitutes true human welfare. In fact the world-view can be visualised as a sieve which filters out the technologies not in consonance with it and thus, in a manner quite akin to Darwinian evolution, the type of technology which survives is the one which has traits in conformity with the world-view.

If we analyse modern technology in this light it emerges that the root cause of various probems associated with modern technology lies in the fact that in the free-market society of the west the technology assessment has been reduced to a mere profit and loss analysis, with no importance given to social, environmental and moral consequences of adoption of a technology. If technology has to be an agent for promoting human welfare, clearly its evaluation should be done on the basis of a proper understanding of what constitutes integral human welfare. Economic welfare is only a very small constituent of integral human welfare, and giving pre-eminent importance to this is the result of currently prevailing Epcicurean world view which equates human welfare with "eat, drink and be merry". It is the tacit adoption of this world

view by the technologists and society at large that is responsible for evolution and exponential growth of modern industrial technology with all its "undesirable" consequences,[6] which are then labelled as acts of social irresponsibility. To bring home the connection between this world view and technology, as an example, it may be mentioned that it does make economic sense to throw away toxic affluents into rivers and poisonous gases into the atmosphere since any attempts at their treatment would only eat into the profits. Similarly, it does make economic sense to perpetuate international wars since this would ensure demand for weapons produced in the "developed" nations. Clearly, if such acts are termed as "socially irresponsible" then society has to agree to change its world-view from its present crass materialistic vision to a more holistic world view which recognises, besides the basic physiological (animal) needs (like food, clothing, shelter, security *etc.*) the higher needs of man *viz.* the various social, moral and spiritual needs. Assessment of technology on the basis of such a holistic view of human welfare would automatically result in the evolution of a humane technology, just as pure economic evaluation has resulted in modern industrial technology. As discussed at length elsewhere[7], such a technology would not only be "socially responsible" but also "morally righteous."

What needs to be done ?

Clearly, what needs to be done in order to inculcate social and moral responsibility in technologists is to bring about this change in world-view. We in India have traditionally cherished the deeper holistic vision of human welfare which was unfortunately abdicated (over last few centuries of foreign subjugation) in favour of a shallower materialistic vision. Fortunately, in the last few decades, it is slowly being realised even in the West that the materialistic vision is in error and that the society should move towards a holistic world-view. Such a transformation can be accomplished only through a massive "adult re-education" programme and a complete revamping of our education system from its present preponderant orientation towards procuring jobs to understanding the "phenomenon of Man." This would also need supplementing the "physical

and "practical" training to develop such traits as concentration, dispassion and equanimity of mind in the face of severe challenges. Such a training is all the more important today in a world of rapid technological change so that our young technologists do not feel overwhelmed by the sheer rapidity of change and are able to discriminate between the "pleasant" and "truly beneficial" technologies. Only such mentally mature technologists can be expected to rise above their physiological impulses and adopt a holistic way of life which is a pre-requisite to evolution of socially responsible technologies.

Concluding Remarks

Quite often, the enormity of this task of changing the world-view forces us to look for some softer options like prescribing some do's and don'ts to ensure that technology remains socially responsible. It is high time that, in the light of above discussions, we recognise the futility of such endeavours. In fact, if the "virus" of materialism is not checked quickly, it will 'enfeeble' the society to such an extent that it may become impossible to bring about this change.

Orient abounds in variety of scientific techniques to improve mental skills and successful application of some of these techniques have been reported in literature.[8] This mental training can prepare the base for adoption of a holistic vision of life. Scientists and technologists trained with such a background will naturally evolve socially and morally responsible technologies.

REFERENCES

1. ELLUL, JACQUES (1965) : *The Technological Society*, Jonathan Cape, London, p. 37.
2. MUMFORD, LEWIS (1934) : *Technics and Civilisation*, Routledge and Kegan Paul Ltd., London, p. 85.
3. GANDHI, M.K. : Quoted in *PPST Bulletin*, Vol. 3, No. 1 May (1983) PPST Group, Madras, p. 3-11.
4. MUM FORD, LEWIS : *op. cit.*, p. 153.

5. COMMONER, BARRY (1972): "On the Meaning of Ecological failures in International Development" in the *Carless Technology* Edited by M.T, Farvar and J.P. Milton, The Natural History Press, Garden City, NY.
6. DHAR, P.L, and R.R. GAUR (1985): "Technology and the Crisis in the West" *Gandhi Marg*, No. 82 January, p. 672-68.
7. DHAR P.L. (1988) : "Holistic Technology—A Conceptual Framework", *Gandhi Marg*, No. 108, March, p. 755-763.
8. VIPASSANA JOURNAL (1985) : Published by Vipassana Vishodhana Vinyas, Bombay (Sec. Ed.) 1985.

7 Systems Methodology and Planning for Social Responsibility of Scientists, Technologists and Managements

P.S. Satsangi*

The Framework for Systems Engineering

Systems engineering has three major dimensions. The time dimension of systems engineering includes the gross sequences or phases that are characteristic of system and extends from the initial conception of an idea through system retirement or phaseout. The logic dimension deals with the steps that are carried out at each of the systems engineering phases. The knowledge dimension refers to specialized knowledge from various professions and disciplines. These are the dimensions of the Hall (1969) morphological box of systems engineering : they are illustrated in Fig. 1.

* Professor, Electrical Engineering Department, I.I.T. Delhi.

The Hall Activity Matrix and Planning

The primary tasks of management are planning, organizing, evaluating, and communicating. In order to conduct these management tasks effectively, one needs a clear statement and understanding of objectives and the interrelations among objectives. Also needed is a method of determining priorities for the objectives based upon their relative merit and the costs of implementing them. Thus the need for a value system is evident.

Four components of the programme planning phase are shown in Table 1. The definition of a goal is the normative component—a statement of what ought to be.

TABLE 1

Four Components of Programme Planning

1.	Definition of a goal	Normative
2.	Knowledge of current position with respect to goal	Descriptive
3.	Knowledge of environmental factors influencing the past, present, and future	Horizon
4.	Determination of best policy given (1), (2), (3)	Analytic

Knowledge of our current position with respect to the goal is the descriptive component—what is, knowledge of all environmental factors influencing the past, present, and future is the planning horizon—what time. Determination of the best policy (optimization) from the goal definition, knowledge of the current state, and knowledge of the environment and time frame is the analytic component—what to do and how.

Some characteristics commonly associated with objectives are : goals, results (events), activities, constraints, and measurements. Objectives can be posed as activities as well as or even independent of results (events). In a hierarchy we would generally see axiological objectives (goals) at the top of the hierarchy, policies (or activities) at the bottom, and various realities in between, as in Fig. 2 (Sage, 1977).

There are two reasons for placing an objective "below" another in an objectives graph, [Fig.3] (Sage, 1977).

1. If objective B necessarily must be attained in order to attain objective A, then objective B is placed below objective A in the structure.
2. If objective C, either separately or in combination with other objectives, represents one alternative way of accomplishing objective A, C lies below A in the structure.

Programme Planning Linkages

The four problem definition variables are: needs, alterables, constraints, and societal sector.

Value System Design

An objective graph or intent structure for the programme in question will be the end result of this effort. Objectives and measures will be given emphasis since they are needed in order to determine success or failure with respect to achieving stated goals.

Philosophers partition value into two levels ; instrumental, or extrinsic value and intrinsic value.

Valuation by money is an example of extrinsic valuation ; the emphasis is not upon the thing but upon the extrinsic properties (money). On the other hand, intrinsic values are qualities that are good in themselves and do not depend upon anything else for their value. Goodness, truth, happiness, and beauty are classic examples of intrinsic value. Intrinsic values are matters of taste or style. Thus extrinsic values are associated with means used to attain the ends in life, whereas intrinsic values are associated with the basic ends themselves. Interestingly, intrinsic values do not decrease as they are used, but often increase, whereas extrinsic values are diminished as items possessing extrinsic values are consumed. In most traditional business and management planning extrinsic values are given much more consideration than intrinsic values. (Sage, 1977).

Thus we see that to value something is to appraise the worth of an object, event, or condition. Axiology is the philosophical study of value. Great philosophical arguments exist concerning whether the important factors influencing values are primarily subjective or objective. There are two principal

branches of axiology. Ethics deals with goodness and badness in a moral sense, whereas aesthetics deals with values in the domain of beauty and the fine arts.

In complex public and societal systems, a decision-maker must frequently allocate resources among system elements which compete for the same resources. If we denote these as elements E_1 and E_2, for example, it is likely that some will place intrinsic valuations upon E_1 and some upon E_2. It is also likely that the decision-maker has little background or knowledge of E_1 and E_2. The evaluation of E_1 and E_2 by the decision-maker can often be enhanced by an instrumental or extrinsic valuation.

Value is a relative term which is associated with various alternatives in a decision analysis problem. Value system will be used to refer to the set of interacting elements which provides a basis for decision-making.

Value system design is therefore construed to be the transformation of the properties of a thing into a format amenable to instrumental or extrinsic valuation.

Allocation of resources represents a value judgement. If we can characterize the value judgment in a manner that relates to human capabilities and human needs, then the judgement is amenable to reasoned criticism. Consider a hypothetical crisis (Sage, 1977) such as black clouds of polluting smoke dominating the environment in a typical industrial small town which has much of its population employed by the polluting industry. If we dispose of the industry, the workers move on to other areas and the pollution problem is resolved. This solution does not relate to human capabilities and needs, although it rids the town of the pollution. The value judgement implied in the example is specifically a decision to eliminate pollution and thus eliminate much of the town's population. Structurally, there were no alternative solutions postulated and no valuation was exercised, extrinsic or intrinsic.

The conclusion of the process of value judgement is the decision. Decision is the expression of preference for a particular outcome from a class of outcomes. If a value judgement is an expression of preference, a proposed judgement which offers only one outcome must therefore be considered

improper and incomplete, since preference implies comparison and this requires two or more class members. In the example just cited, the crisis was transformed into the objective "to get rid of the pollution." There were no constraints, although these would be obvious if the objective has been "to reestablish the town to its environmental and economic status before pollution took over." The latter objective offers alternative scenarios such as the economic and social functioning of the town in the past, present, and future. The systems engineer can assist the decision-maker in constructing scenarios, structuring alternative solutions, developing procedures for reaching decisions, and communication of value judgements.

Societal value judgements are frequently difficult to discuss because such topics are often perceived in two simultaneous categories, subjective and objective.

The treatment of subjective topics using objective methodologies is the principal goal of value system design. In fact, systemic methodologies can be exercised in an iterative fashion to arrive at value judgements more palatable to the subjectivist. The objectivistic approach to the value system design portion of programme planning consists primarily of identifying. The identification of an objective or activity implies that it is possible to obtain value from the attainment of the objective or the pursuit of the activity. Selection of given objectives or activities to the exclusion of others is a value claim by the selector.

One objective in value system design is defining objectives, obtaining an intent structure of them, and ordering them in a hierarchical structure as in Fig. 3.

It is also very helpful to relate the objectives to the problem definition linkages of needs, alterables, constraints, and societal sectors, as indicated in Fig. 4.

In programme planning, the value system design activity consists of three distinct features :

1. Defining objectives and ordering them in a hierarchical structure.
2. Relating the objectives to needs, constraints and alterables.

3. Defining a set of measures by which to determine attainment of the objectives.

The ordering of objectives is accomplished using subordination matrix and the transitive relation "How" and/or "Why". Definition of the objectives is obtained from group and stakeholder community dialogue. The needs, alterables, and constraints are obtained from the problem definition step. The topic of measures is expanded to include the measures of both objectives and activities, as the same discussion is pertinent to both.

Selection of relevant sets of measures for objectives and activities is a portion of the value system design and system synthesis steps, respectively. The needs, alterables, constraints, objectives, and activities interaction matrices supply a set of elements with which the measure of objectives and activities can be deduced. A set of objectives measures should be visible to all persons involved, from the policy-maker to the operations level.

The final step in value system design consists of defining a set of objectives measures to measure attainment of objectives.

System Synthesis

The system synthesis step is concerned primarily with the answers to three questions : What are the alternative approaches for attaining each objective ? How is each alternative approach described ? How do we measure attainment of each alternative approach ? The answers to these three questions lead to a series of activities and a set of activities measures.

The linkages of objectives, activities, activities measures, objectives measures, and objectives is the system synthesis portion of programme planning. System synthesis is the combining of the elements into a whole. The creation of the activities is a portion of synthesis as well as an application of value judgment.

Figure 4 (Sage, 1977) presents the programme planning linkages, which consist of the problem definition, value system design, and system synthesis steps. The systemic methodology

of unified programme planning offers a format for the product of the planning effort which is amenable to modification and expansion. It offers visibility to the planning process. Needs, alterables, and constraints are represented and linked as they were in the problem definition step.

The objectives measures, activities, and activity measures are developed to satisfy the intentions expressed by the system objectives.

Interpretive Structural Modelling (ISM)

The ISM process represented by model exchange isomorphisms in Fig.5 (Sage 1977) transforms unclear poorly articulated mental models of systems into visible well-defined models useful for many purposes (such as value system design). An interpretive two structural model of social responsibility for scientists, technologists and managers as presented in (Satsangi *et al*, 1988).

REFERENCES

ANDREW P. SAGE (1977) : *Methodology for Large Scale Systems*, McGraw Hill, New York.

HALL, A.D. (1969) : "Three Dimension Morphology of Systems Engineering IEEEG-SSC Transactions, Vol. 5, No. 2, pp. 156-160.

P.S. SATSANGI, L.M. Chalpa A. Chandramoli, Raka Sharan (1988) in A. Shanmagasundaram and M.C. Mathur (Eds.) *Recent Trands in Applied System Research*, Popular Publishing House, New Delhi pp. 210-283.

of unified programmatic planning efforts is outlined so as to produce [illegible] planning effort which is amenable to [illegible] and expansion. [illegible] efforts with [illegible] planning process [illegible] alternatives [illegible] and [illegible] were in the program [illegible] step.

The objectives, measures, activities, and activity measures are [illegible] to study the alterations [illegible] by the [illegible] objectives.

Interpretive Structural Modelling (ISM)

The ISM process represented by model exchange is [illegible] in Fig 3 (Sage 1977) transforms unclear poorly articulated mental models of systems into visible well-defined models useful for many purposes such as value system design. An interpretive structural model of social responsibility for scientists, technologists and managers is presented in [illegible] et al., 1988).

REFERENCES

ANDREW P. SAGE (1977). *Methodology for Large Scale Systems*, McGraw Hill, New York.

HALL, A.D. (1969). "Three Dimensional Morphology of Systems Engineering", IEEE-SSC Transactions, Vol. [illegible], No. 2, pp. [illegible].

[illegible] SATSANGI, P.S. [illegible] Chadha [illegible] A. Shanmugasundaram and M. [illegible] (1988) [illegible] *Applied System Research*, Popular Publishing House, New Delhi, pp. 210-[illegible].

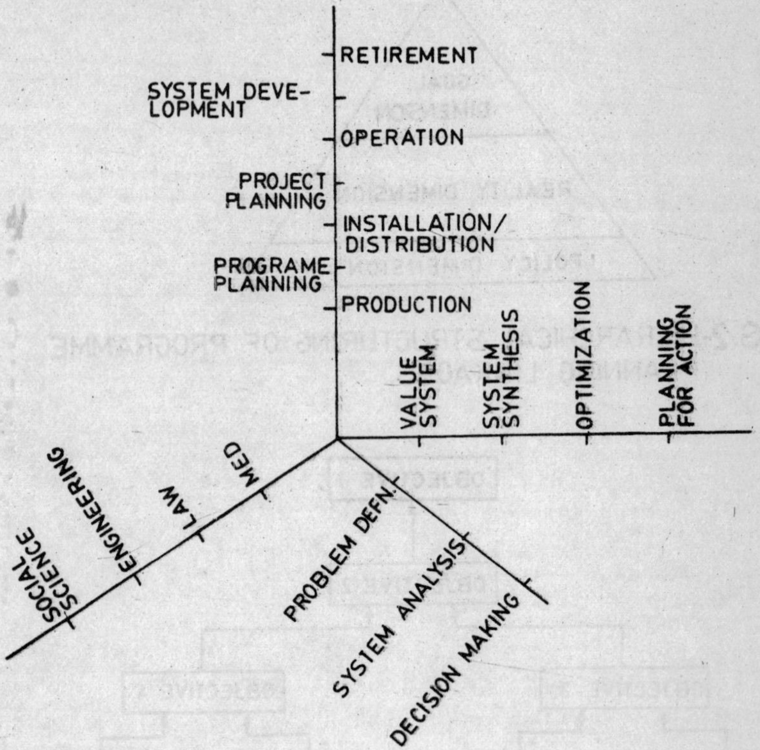

FIG. 1-THREE DIMENSIONAL SYSTEMS ENGINEERING FRAMEWORK

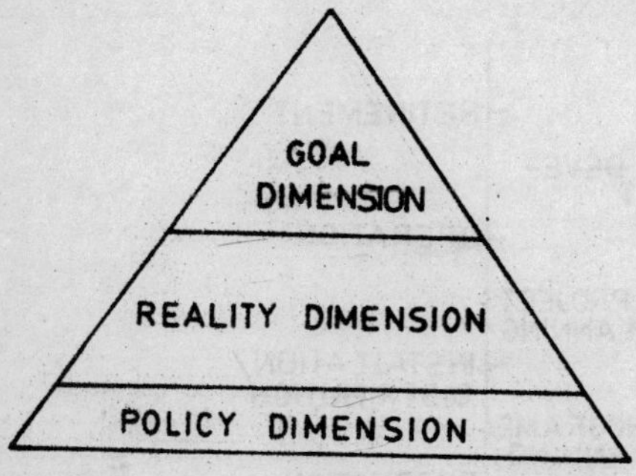

FIG. 2-HIERARCHICAL STRUCTURING OF PROGRAMME PLANNING LINKAGES

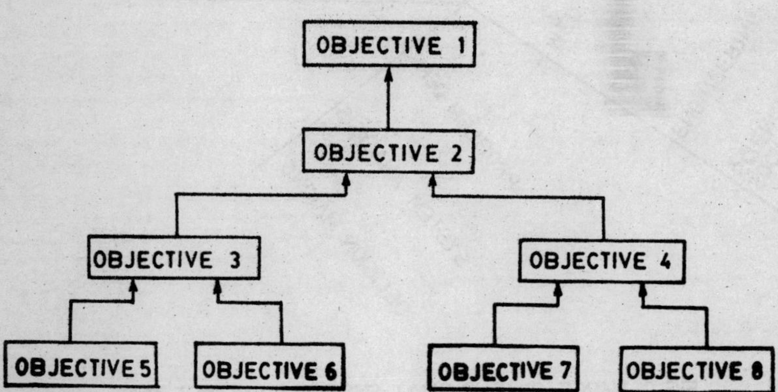

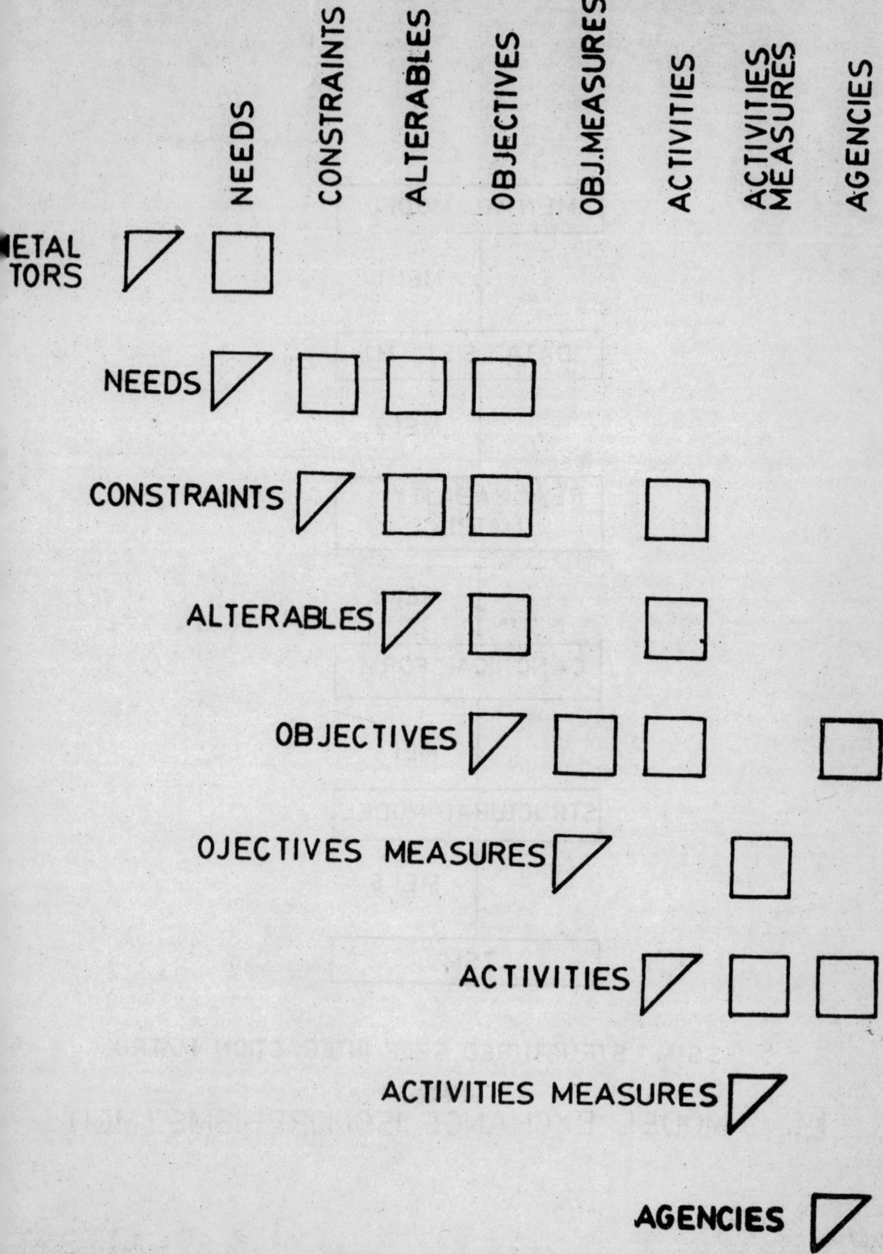

FIG.4-PROGRAM PLANNING LINKAGES

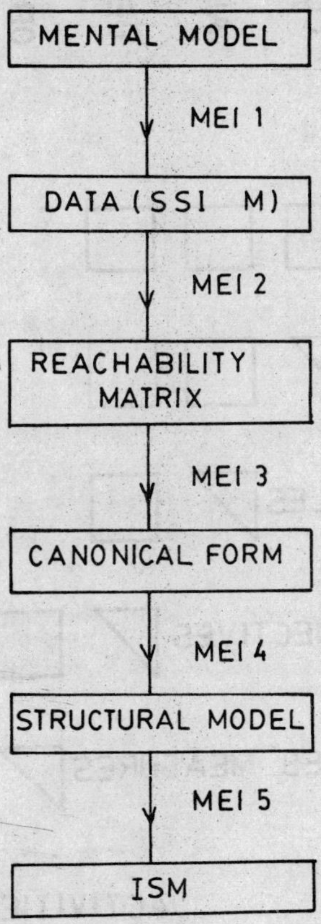

SSIM : STRUCTURED SELF INTERACTION MATRIX

FIG. 5-MODEL EXCHANGE ISOMORPHISMS (MEI)

8 | Bureaucracy and Society : Limitations, Responsibilities and Constraints

Nivedita Haran* and Raka Sharan**

Introduction

Literally the word bureaucracy means "a government of bureaux or desks", *i.e.*, a government where decisions are taken sitting at desks. A 'desk government' should in reality denote forethought, planning, analysis of facts, decisions, direction and co-ordination on a rational basis of performance and assurance of results. It implies contribution of the mind, knowledge and insight, all of which are highly desirable. Sometimes a desk also has certain unpleasant connotations, such as, rigid adherence to rules, absence of field experience and tendency to generalise. It is because these aspects of bureaucracy come to the fore more often than its more positive qualities that the word has become more of an abuse. However, bureaucracy describes a particular system of administration. Historically it was associated with the rule of government

* Civil Servant and a Part-time Research Scholar at the I.I.T., Delhi.

**Faculty member in the Department of Humanities and Social Sciences, IIT, Delhi.

and governmental officials ; but sociologists regard it as a form of administration that is found in organizations pursuing a wide variety of goals to create a balance structure of power. It is, however, governmental bureaucracy that makes and implements public policies, in consultation with the political parties and interest groups. Amidst the fluctuating fortunes of parties and the groups bureaucracy provides administrative expertise and stability. Despite its having a bad connotation, bureaucracy has come to acquire a vital role and enormus power in modern governments.

In recent time various scholars/social scientists have shown interest in studying the bureaucracy of different societies. Most of the social scientists who have studied bureaucracy, have tried to analyse the interim role, structure and formation of bureaucracy. They have ignored to understand the role of bureaucracy as an agent of social transformation. In this paper we are trying to discuss the responsibilities of Indian bureaucracy in the process of generating a social change in Indian society. Whenever one talks of responsibilities one should not forget to analyse the constraints incorporated in them. Therefore, this paper has tried to focus its attention on the aspects of constraints and the limitations also.

The paper is divided into three sub-sections. The first section deals with the theoretical framework of bureaucracy, the second section presents the role and responsibilities of Indian bureaucracy in a historical framework and the last section deals with the constraints in the process of social-transformation brought about by bureaucratic organization and some concluding remarks on them.

I

CONCEPT AND THEORETICAL FRAMEWORK

Bureaucracy is an ambiguous term which might mean :

(a) the type of organisation used by modern government for conduct of its various specialised functions, embodied in the administrative system and personified by the Civil Service.

(b) a mechanistic and formal approach in carrying out

such functions with complete indifference towards the effects achieved.

(c) the kind of government that shoulders a large burden of responsibilities especially in the economic and social spheres.

(d) a political condition in which the executive branch plays a role increasingly more important than the legislative and judicial branches.

(e) a government subject to control not by the electorate but by a group of power-hungry functionaries.

(f) according to a meaning prevalent in the second half of the nineteenth century in Germany, a bureaucratically organised society was one directed by a civil servant who alone was responsible for his subordinates' action. This meaning had a strong suggestion of efficiency.

(g) it is a structure manned by trained personnel who are grouped in specific command relationships and with a common goal.

It is (a) and (g) along with (b) which convey the more familiar and recent meaning.

The best point of departure for understanding the theoretical framework of bureaucracy is to begin with, Max Weber's notion on "ideal type bureaucracy", Max Weber's characterization of bureaucracy has been summed up in terms of the following :

(1) A continuous organization of official functions bound by rules.

(2) A specific sphere of competence, and a sphere of obligations to perform functions which have been marked-off as part of a systematic division of labour, and the provision of the incumbent with the necessary authority to carry out these functions.

(3) The organization of office follows the principles of hierarchy, *i.e.*, each lower office is under the control and supervision of a higher one.

(4) The rules which regulate the conduct of an office may

be technical rules or norms. In such cases, if their application is to be fully rational, specialized training is necessary. It is thus normally true that only a person who has demonstrated an adequate technical training is qualified to be a member of the administrative staff.

(5) It is a matter of principle that the members of the administrative staff should be completely separated from ownership of the means of production or administration. There exists, furthermore in principle, complete separation of property belonging to the organization, which is controlled within the spheres of the office, and the personal property of an official.

(6) Administrative acts, decisions and rules are formulated and recorded in writing.

Thus official duties, a specific sphere of competence, hierarchical division of authority, technical rules, separation of management from ownership ; official position as incumbency rather than as property or inheritance, and documentary recording of administrative acts, are the elements of bureaucracy. These elements are generally absent from the feudal or traditional forms of administration in which heredity and status, personal relations, and the overlap of personal and public spheres of activities are prominent. In summary form, bureaucracy has the following characteristics :

(i) fixed and official jurisdictional areas, which are regularly ordered by rules, that is by laws or administrative regulations ;

(ii) principles of hierarchy and levels of graded authority that ensure a firmly ordered system in which higher offices supervise lower ones ;

(iii) administration based upon written documents. The body of officials engaged in handling these documents and files, along with other materials apparatus, make up a 'bureau' or 'office' ;

(iv) administration by full time officials who are thoroughly and expertly trained ; and

(v) administration by general rules which are quite stable and comprehensive.

Max Weber's conceptualization of bureaucracy is based on his notion of rationality. Weber classifies authority into three types—traditional, charismatic and rational. Traditional authority is based on birth and status without reference to technical merit. Traditional authority is an inheritance and an ascribed property. In a traditional society, status defines role rather than role determining status. Charismatic authority is inherent in outstanding individual endowed with extraordinary personal magnetism. Such individuals are rare leaders, generally produced in time of crisis. Rational authority, on the other hand, is to be found in formal organizations where individuals hold office on merit or expert qualification for specific jobs, and are judged by their performance rather than by their personal or official status. Rational authority inheres in office rather than in the incumbent as an individual. According to Max Weber, bureaucracy, based as it is on merit or technical qualification, formal duties and impersonal rules and relationships, represents the development of rationality human organizations.

Weber argues that bureaucracy is not only characterized by rational authority but is also endowed with technical superiority and is, therefore, conducive to efficiency. An obvious merit of ideal bureaucracy is a concern for objectivity and impartiality. Bureaucratic decisions are ideally based not on personal considerations but on formal rules. The objective discharge of business primarily means the discharge of business according to calculable rules and 'without regard for persons'.

In Weber's scheme, however, there is a confusion between the elements and the consequences of bureaucratic organization. Blau and Scott rightly point out that Weber's construct of bureaucracy is an admixture of a conceptual scheme and a set of hypotheses. Weber's ideal type comprises the key elements of bureaucratic organization. Whether these consequences follow from the elements of bureaucratic organization or not is an open question and can only have the status of a

hypothesis. For example, whether administrative efficiency results from bureaucratic rationality or not, is an empirical, not a logical question. The question regarding the extent to which rationality is an essential or exclusive element in a bureauratic organization may also be posed here.

The artificiality and confusion of the ideal type are properly exposed where considering the dysfunctions of the various elements of bureaucracy, and the conflicts that may arise among these elements. In this connection Merton's exposition of bureaucratic dysfunctions is illuminating. He considers the negative aspects of bureaucracy through the application of Weber's concept of 'trained incapacity', which refers to the state of affairs in which one's abilities function as inadequacies. For the successful operation of bureaucracy, a high degree of reliability of behaviour and of conformity is necessary. However, Merton points out that as 'adherence to the rules originally conceived as a means becomes transformed into an end in itself, there occurs the familiar process of displacement of goals whereby an instrumental value becomes a terminal value. Discipline, readily interpreted as conformity with regulations, whatever the situation, is seen not as a measure designed for a specific purpose, but as an immediate value in the life-organization of the bureaucrat.

Such formalism and rigidity, according to Merton, derive from structural sources. There is a need for discipline and devotion to formal rules as means is turned into the observing of rules as an end. Such rigidity regarding rules interferes with spontaneous adaptation under special conditions. Thus the very elements that are expected to rationalize bureaucratic behaviour and enhance its efficiency in routine matters may produce inefficiency in special instances and circumstances.

Another dysfunctional aspect of bureaucracy pertains to the rise of defence mechanisms of an informal order which tend to arise whenever there is a threat to the integrity of a group. The bureaucrats tend to develop a sense of a common destiny and an esprit d' corps. They share and defend their entrenched interests above everything else. The stress and 'depersonalization of relationships' further builds a barrier between the bureaucratic official and the mass of the people. The bureau-

cratic official representing the power and the prestige of government, with his own image of merit and impartiality, is likely to develop an arrogant and superior attitude in sharp contrast to his theoretical self-description as public servant.

As against Weber's emphasis on formal rules and impersonal conduct in bureaucracy, others have drawn attention to the importance of informal interactions, unofficial transactions, and friendship patterns.

II

HISTORICAL BACKGROUND (ROLES & RESPONSIBILITIES)

Till the Mughal period there was no well-established system of administrative bureaucracy worth the name in India. On the one hand there were the representatives of kings who collected revenue from the people, and on the other, there was the ubiquitous army who though not concerned with day-to-day administration were always at hand. With the arrival of the British and subsequently the introduction of the Indian Civil Service a well-knit hierarchical structure came into being. The British interest was to hold India without creating any unnecessary discontent. The cost of administration was kept at a minimum. Enactment of new legislations, unless unavoidable, was not resorted to. Officers toured extensively, met people, inspected offices, estimated the efficiency of their subordinates and provided guidance whenever necessary. But their first and foremost task was to maintain law and order. The legislations enacted and developmental schemes undertaken were aimed at improving the prestige of the colonial power and to create goodwill for future exigencies.

With Independence there was a shift in priorities and goals. Maintaining law and order now did not imply keeping in check patriotic and rebellious spirit but ensuring communal harmony. The main tasks of bureaucracy now was to implement the plethora of new schemes and programmes all aimed at alleviating poverty and bringing about economic development. This has led to a wider concern among the academician. Interest has been shown by the Indian social scientists to study

nature, structure and role of Indian bureaucracy. Recently a few studies have been conducted by a few eminent scholars such as D.N. Rao and R.K. Trivedi (1961), V. Subramanian (1967), V. Jagannathan and A.P. Barnabas (1968, 1969) C.P. Bhandari (1970), S.K. Kshir Sagar (1968, 1971), C.P. Bhambri (1971), A.R. Tyagi (1971), K.K. Singh and Ali Ashraf (1971), V.A. Pai Panandikar (1973), K. Mathur (1973), G.K. Prasad (1974), H.K. Singhi (1974). Most of these studies deal with matters like bureaucratic profiles, bureaucratic attitudes, relationship with citizens, relation and influence of politics, and satisfaction of a bureaucrat towards his job.

Singhi (1974) analyses the role structure, interactions and value orientations of bureaucrats in Rajasthan. He has investigated the governmental and non-governmental sector. His starting point has been Weber's classical formulation and coming to the dysfunctional aspects of the organization he takes into account Parsons's scheme of system-sub-system analysis. He concludes : the present day bureaucratic system weighs too heavily in favour of routine administrative tasks and is unsuitable for the achievement of goals of national development. In a traditional society with historically rigid stratified social system, the bureaucratic organization tends to have greater caste-like structure. The bureaucratic system has concentration of authority and decision-making in the hands of elite cadre primarily oriented to order and tends to be power-oriented.

Dube (1974 : 71-96) talks about bureaucracy's importance in nation-building. Further, he describes the role of bureaucracy in economic development. Bureaucracy can make a contribution to the process of economic development as (i) it has to provide infrastructure for economic development, (ii) it has to prepare blueprints for economic development and devices for their effective implementation, (iii) it has to assess and evaluate the results of its efforts. Taking into account these functions. Dube emphasises the dysfunctions and pathological shortcoming of a bureaucratic organization in newly independent countries with special reference to India. He says that the four main attributes of bureaucracy, *i.e.* efficiency, predictability, impersonalization and rationality are not

operative in the Indian situation. India inherited a civil service tradition which has undergone a lot of change over the years. But the situation after the independence has changed and the bureaucracy is facing a lot of problems.

III

RESPONSIBILITIES AND CONSTRAINTS OF INDIAN BUREAUCRACY

The Internal World

The members of the bureaucratic system are also members of a social system, culture, such as those exemplified by family and kinship, religion, caste, language and region, socio-economic status and so on. Before entering the service between the age of 23 and 26, they are part of a social milieu having their own position on the socio-economic scale. Experience shows that a majority of the entrants to the service come from a middle or higher middle class background. (No study across the years has perhaps been conducted on the changing pattern, if any, of the socio-economic background of fresh bureaucrats). Again a sizeable chunk of the seats reserved for SCs and STs are also cornered by those belonging to the higher economic status, such as wards of civil servants, ministers, other politicians, *etc.* The candidates from the weaker sections and who are also economically backward, given their in-built handicap, of lack of exposure, lack of opportunities, and lesser competition in schools and colleges in rural areas stand an extremely slim chance of being successful.

With the increasing involvement of bureaucrats in selection, implementation and evaluation of development-oriented programmes the hiatus between them and members of the public has narrowed. Bureaucrates these days have to be approachable and available. The task of implementing developmental activity which the bureaucracy is entrusted with requires changing the socio-economic system, where he is working, from within. He has to have first-hand knowledge of the life of the

common people, and must empathise with them to make implementation of these schemes a success. The 'demi-god' of yesterday has to now shed his aloofness and go to the masses. He needs lessons in public relations, crowd management, and of course socio-religious information of the people and the area where he is working.

Gone are the days when the civil servant could spend his entire career in his ivory tower, without meeting the people or learning the language. Although it was said earlier that the bureaucrat of the pre-Independence era perhaps toured more than their counterparts now do, the touring was often due to purely academic reasons many officers of that period produced historical and sociological works on the people of that region, flora, fauna, living conditions and so on. Thus Loggan perhaps wrote his voluminous Manual not because he wanted to find out which poverty alleviation programme would be best suited to that region and or to design one but because he wanted to leave behind a record for posterity.

But for tody's bureaucrat the goals are different. Very few, if any, treat a field posting as a source of academic pursuits. They would rather innovate new schemes for ensuring quicker and better socio-economic development of that area.

Corresponding to the change in role of the bureaucrat the people's attitude too has undergone a change. Having become more aware of their rights people have come to demand more. Often bureaucratic decisions are challenged through direct petitions and even appeals.

The Constraints of the External World

Earlier we discussed the internal world of a bureaucrats. In contrast to this internal world, there is also what for the sake of simplicity one might call his external world'. By 'external world' we mean the network of political system within which he functions, the innumerable legislations which determine his actions and of course, the traditional bureaucratic culture which exists in a given society. There is a legal and constitutional role he is constrained to play. Let us enumerate some these functions :

(i) Bureaucracy has to provide services and technical advice and guidance in respect of making resources available for developmental activity,

(ii) It has to provide the feedback mechanism taking into consideration the aspirations and demands of the community,

(iii) Coordination between different developmental activities and between developmental and *pre se* non-developmental activities must also be ensu ed,

(iv) Bureaucrats must maintain adequate link with the people's representatives and yet not be unduly influenced by them, and

(v) Bureaucracy has also to facilitate change in attitudes and approaches of the people, of political representative and at times even his colleagues and superiors.

Thus, bureaucracy is simultaneously called upon to ensure maximum degree of stability, promote societal integration, facilitate economic development, collect revenue for the government and also make it possible to bring about structural changes through a more equitable system of distribution. This indeed is a tall order and requires an unimpeachable moral fibre, missionary zeal and physical strength. The bureaucrat of today has to be an administrator-manager-missionary rolled into one. Yet the constraints faced by him are many more today than even before.

Conflict

If the job-structure of a bureaucrat is analysed these appear a number of conflict areas which by their very presence inhibit and decelerate his functioning.

First, the conflict situation arising from the individual's socio-econmic background before he entered the service and the demands of the job. From an ego-centric existence he is suddenly plunged into a world of service. It is only for some that the primary aim in choosing this career is to serve the people : often it is the lure for power, authority and fame, (notwithstanding the fact that even during the initial training he is again and again told how important anonymity is for a bureaucrat). But how does one ensure that the new recruits are "service-oriented". Our educational system does not always successfuly imbibe it in us. And ironically those genuinely interested in social service prefer to do it on their own without entering government service.

The second conflict situation arises from the legally defined role of a bureaucrat and the soaring demands of the people. The increasing aspirations of the citizens act as a double-edged sword. While on the one hand it ensures continuous pressure on the political leaders and bureaucrats to give the people their due, it also makes the bureaucrats' job more difficult. Ensconsed in a governmental politico-social set-up where he is answerable to the elected bosses, the bureaucrat is also the closet link with the people. The local SDM or Collector has no locus standi to contradict and to convince the people about their impracticality. The bureaucrat thus is caught amidst the demands for social justice and equality by the people supported by the politicians and the statutory limitations within which he is to act in addition to the limited resources.

Third is the psychological conflict arising from the sky-high expectations in terms of power and perks by the new entrant and the limitations of rules and regulations which if strictly interpreted often leave him quite bereft of dicisional power. For, in all our rules, the element of discrimination is minimal. But, interpretations vary.

These conflict areas are created due to the vastly varying role perceptions which arise due to varying socio-cultural milieu. It is the educational training and social upbringing of a person which leads him to expect from the service that which is not fact-based. Again, the demands of the public are guided more by emotion than by a rational analysis based on resource availability, the legal provisions and the socio-cultural background.

Added to these are the general drop in moral values which has led to more corruption, less commitment and cut-throat competition. For in a society where financial status is the yardstick of success and prosperity, the bureaucrat has also been affected by it. Gone are the days of anonymity ; often bureaucrats vie with each other to grab choice postings. Success in service is measured in terms of the number of "foreign trips" undertaken at government's expense. Routine jobs are shunned, emphasis is on "drives" and protocol jobs which attract publicity. Of late there has also been the tendency to

introduce "new schemes" with catchy names, and often the only thing new about such schemes are their names.

Conclusion

The following observations are made by way of suggestions :

(i) There is necessity for prescribing a change in personality type for the new-recruit bureaucrat. To begin with, more recruits should be drawn from the lower and lower middle economic strata. Here a presumption is made that a person from a less affluent background can empathise with the rural masses better, which may, however, be unwarranted.

(ii) The training programmes, including orientation courses, should be re-devised and improvised. They should aim at equipping the bureaucrat to handle new tasks. The emphasis should be not only on formal training and imparting of information and knowledge but also creating new awareness about the importance of working with the people which is essential for the success of all developmental programmes. It should, in other words, resocialise the new entrant.

(iii) A sense of service cannot be developed by a training programme alone. For that the education system should also be a contributory factor. Education should teach not only what one can get from a particular career but also what one has to give in return.

(iv) Decentralised planning and devolution of powers to local agencies can help prevent concentration of power and responsibilities. Local people will then have a direct hand in selection of projects.

(v) The political representatives play a role in educating the people. The people should not be encouraged to make irrational demands. In this our academicians and social service voluntary organisations should also be involved. For it is an extremely difficult task to bring down expectations.

(vi) Greater emphasis should be placed on the human relations approach within bureaucracy rather than its emphasis on hierarchy.

(vii) High level expert bureaux may be set up in key sectors, drawing also from non-governmental organisations (NGOs)

(viii) New operating cultures within administration may be encouraged. These do not have to be borrowed from outside ; they should emerge from a creative response to the challenges of the contemporary social reality.

REFERENCES

BENDIX, REINHARD, (1974) : *Nation-Building and Citizenship* ; New Delhi, Willey, pp. 106-42.

BLAU, PETER M. (1955) : *Dynamics of Bureaucracy*; London, Chicago Press.

——(1974) : *On the nature of Organizations*, New York, John Willey.

CRUISE O' BRIEN, DONAL B. (1977) : "A Versatile Charisma : The Mouride Brotherhood : 1967-75." *European Journal of Sociology*, Vol. 18 (1), pp. 83-106.

DAMLE, Y.B., "A Framework for the Study of Bureaucracy" in *Public Services and Social Responsibility*, Ed. S.C. Dube, Vikas.

DE, NITISH R., Bureaucracy : Obsolescence and Innovation in *Public Service and Social Responsibility* Ed. S.C. Dube.

DUBE, S.C., (1974) : *Contemporary India and Its Modernization*, New Delhi, Vikas, pp. 71-96.

HODGETTS, J.E.&Corbett, D.C., (1960) *Canadian Public Adminitstration Book of Readings*.

MERTON, R.K., (1949, 1968) : *Social Theory and Social Structure*, New York : Amrind.

MEYER, MARSHEL, W., and M. CRAIG BROWN, (1977) "The Process of Bureaucratization, *American Journal of Sociology*, Vol. 18 (2) pp. 364-85.

MITCHFLL G. DUNCAN (1968) : *A Dictionary of Sociology*; London Kegan Paul, Vol 2, pp. 10-22.

MURRAY, JAMES A.H. *et al* (1971): *Oxford English Dictionary*; *Oxford* Vol. I pp. 1184, Vol. II, pp. 1126.

PANANDIKAR, V.A. PAL (1973) : *A Survey of Research in Public Administration*, Delhi ICSSR, Vol. I, p. 17-22.

SHANKAR, R. (1976), "Bureaucracy, Review of Literature with Special Reference to Latin America" Seminar Paper.

9 Social Responsibility of Education

A. Shekhar*

The need for social sensitization of the educated towards serious problems facing our country hardly needs any emphasis. The Greek philosopher, Plato long ago stressed that education must make "reasonable men" for the stability of the state. To him, a reasonable man or a good citizen was one who was conscious of his duties towards the state.[1]

"What is education?" has been a basic question exercising the minds of thinkers in all civilized societies. It has such a wide connotation that its precise definition is not possible. From cultural transmission and training for a good life to self-realization, it has been interpreted in various ways. However, there is no doubt about its significance in the development of individuals and betterment of society. Individually, education enables one to have a proper kind of self-evaluation culminating in "self-actualization". For the society, education enables one to have civic efficiency leading to social development. The individual and social aims of education are, however, not contradictory. On the contrary, the education of individual is best expressed when it is for the betterment of society. Besides

*Research Scholar, Department of Humanities & Social Sciences, I.I.T. Delhi.

this social aim, ideal education seeks to inculcate a spirit of enquiry, creativeness, human values, good character and a broader outlook in the recipient.

Although education is largely shaped by the politico-economic sub-systems of society, its role as a significant agent of social reconstruction cannot be over emphasized. This paper addresses itself to the task of educational reform emphasizing that a greater involvement of the system of education in societal reconstruction for good education is not only a preparation for life but also a training for participation in life around us.

Today our country is passing through one of the most challenging times in history. Its cherished goal of modernization with stability is facing hurdles in the form of superstitious beliefs and practices, poverty and ignorance, communalism and regionalism, which are eating away the vitals of our national fabric. Can the educated and privileged minority of this country remain insensitive to this grave threat for too long? Therefore, there is an urgent need of social awakening towards making an educational policy which can complete the task of societal reconstruction. This paper has tried to take up the issue by way of making a historical and comparative study on the problems of education.

Education in Developed Countries

The USSR and the USA are glaring examples of using formal education as means of transforming their social order.[2] In the case of the USSR, the commitment has been to Marxist-Leninism and education has been used as an indoctrination device. According to Marxists, abilities are acquired and are not innate and that differences between children represent differenees in environmental conditions. Therefore, there is an emphasis on proper care of children in public creches and schools. This also releases the women for work, who enjoy a higher status than women of most of other western countries.

Another special feature of education in USSR is that it combines study with work and every student except the most gifted are given work experience between the ages of 14 and 20. This scheme has been adopted to meet the shortage of

labour and to prevent the isolation of the student from the rest of society.

In USA, John Dewey's philosophy of education has been followed in order to bring the different immigrant groups into an integrated social, economic and cultural order . . . "The American way of life." Education functions as a unifying force. There is provision for common education to all people irrespective of class. The contents of curriculum have been devised to cater to the needs of individual child and cover a wide range of practical and academic skills which the modern community requires.[3] The emphasis is on quality and excellence in all the fields of education.

Education in Developing Countries

The structure of education in developing countries differs from one country to another. Some countries like India and China have a rich cultural heritage. Earlier these countries had a network of village schools attached to local religious places, where mostly religious texts were taught.

Against this background an attempt is now being made in these newly independent countries to evolve a new system of education on the pattern of the developed nations of the west. However, in these countries there is an imperative need to plan education process in the light of local requirements instead of blindly emulating the west because of the inherent differences in the socio-economic, cultural and educational structures of the countries of developing and developed worlds.

The Indian Scenario

The modern Indian education has roots in the education introduced by the Britishers to serve their own colonial interests. Being a foreign importation it is cut-off from the Indian reality and lacks social direction. It has alienated the educated from the socio-economic reality of our country. They get a false notion of superior status and look-down upon the less privileged ones, just like their British predecessors.

The present scene is despite the fact that since independence the country has had three national policies on education—

1968, 1979 and 1986—very concerned with the gravity of the problem. Besides, scores of educational committees and commissions have been suggesting various measures to improve the educational mess in the country. What happened to them would be clear from just one example. As far back as 1944, the Sargeant Plan envisaged introduction of universal, free and compulsory education of all children between the age of 6 to 11 years. This target is still largely unachieved despite Constitu tional directive. Much has been written about the educational commissions and committees so it would be worthwhile to discuss here only the new NEP 1986.

National Education Policy 1986[4]

Like earlier plans, the new policy also takes up the issue with much rhetoric calling the task of educational reform a challenge. It rightly considers education an ingredient for social transformation and an important investment in human resource development. However, a careful analysis of the NEP 1986, makes it clear that it is not so bold and innovative. In fact, it has even abandoned the progressive recommendations of the Kothari Commission (1964-66) e.g., the Common School System and the Neighbourhood School Plan and neglected the Gandhian scheme of 'Basic Education' and work experience. No doubt, the NEP 1986 has laid down some right priorities, when it says that the main task is to strengthen the "base of the pyramid." But its vision gets distorted later when its priorities multiply leading to pick and choose at the administrative level. As for example, the elitist measures of the policy *e.g.*, Model Schools at the secondary level, autonomous colleges and centres of excellence at the higher level of education, perhaps appear more important to the government than 'Operation Blackboard' and vocationalization at all levels of education, which can drastically change the educational scenario of our country. However, they are unlikely to succeed. The former due to the magnitude of the problem vis-a-vis-financial allocation and the latter due to lack of a conductive social environment for vocational courses. Further, it is disappointing to note that in the sphere of education women have not been able to make a proper headway even after the

40 years of independence. In fact, "women's education has not received the due care and attention from the planners and policy makers."[5] This is evident from the Census Report of 1981, which shows that literacy rate for women is only 24.8 per cent while for male it is around 47 per cent. Coming to the field of higher education there has been a phenomenal growth after independence. "This process of unreasonable expansion in its present form has led to many of the ills and corruption within the system and we are face to face with the problem of unemployable graduates."[6]

Therefore, in brief, it may be said about the present educational scene in the country that although there has been quantitative achievement and improvement in quality of life for a few, for the majority of the countrymen the various educational policies and strategies have proved a dismal failure. The elitist bias in education, unrelatedness to life and falling standards, injustice to women, unemployment and student unrest, poor status of teachers and degradation of values have increased with every passing day. Here, serious doubts arise in one's mind, for instance—(1) Have we really sought to restructure education in accordance with our needs ? (2) Have not the educationists acquired a vested interest in education as it obtains today ?

These doubts arise due to the fact that the popularly elected government has, by various experimentations in the field of education, merely tinkered with the problems and situation has gone from bad to worse. The fruits of education have not reached the majority of our countrymen especially women and rural first generation educated youth. In order to improve their lot a "fire-fighting" kind of operation is the need of the hour to remove illiteracy, provide equality of educational opportunity in letter and spirit and more employment oriented education so that they become a healthy unit of our national system.

Here, it would not be out of place to mention Gandhiji's model of education known as *Nai Talim*,[7] as a guideline for educational reform. The great visionary so rightly laid emphasis on inculcating the spirit of self-reliance, self-restraint and bread-labour through education at the primary stage. The

main thrust of his education was that, it should be imparted primarily through crafts like weaving and spinning and not through books only ; so that the children may produce articles that are marketable and these should be sold to make education self-supporting. But this concept of teaching could not get accepted in our society where dignity of labour is not upheld. Even the modified SUPW scheme has been sidetracked in the new policy on education. There is, however, no argument over making education free up to secondary stage for universal and compulsory education but work ethic must be taught to the children. There is an urgent need for social awakening also in order to accommodate such changes in education. J.P. Naik wrote in this regard : "A very persistent effort needs to be made to educate all concerned to realize that a radical reconstruction of education and a socio-economic transformation have to go together."[8] It is high time that our priorities in education be set right. The state should intervene in favour of the masses and give them essential support and protection in order that they overcome their basic handicap of poverty and backwardness. For this purpose an integrated approach should be adopted, *i.e.* "a simultaneous effort to transform society and education in keeping with the national goals of socialism and democracy and the ultimate creation of an egalitarian and non-exploitative society based on justice, equality, freedom and the dignity of the individual."[9]

Besides, our planning process should involve people in programmes of planned educational development. This will create acceptance for the new measures of educational reform. The various media of mass communication can also be effectively used for the popularisation of various schemes. The basic motto should be, as Naik said, "Education through reconstruction and reconstruction through education."[10]

REFERENCES

1. NETTLESHIP, R.L. (ed). (1963) : *Lectures on the Republic of Plato* ; Macmillan.
2. MUKHERJI, L. (1975) : *Comparative Education* ; Allied Publishers.
3. HALSEY, A.H. (1968) : Educational Organisation, *International*

Encyclopedia of the Social Sciences, Vol. 4 ; Macmillan and Free Press.

4. *National Policy on Education*—1986.
5. SHARAN, R. ; "Women's Education in India : A critical Appraisal,"(Unpublished paper).
6. MOHAN, DINESH (1984) : "Travails of Higher Education," *The Times of India* ; New Delhi, 8 November.
7. MUKHERJI, S.N. (1969) : *Education in India :Today and Tomorrow*, Acharya Book Depot.
8. NAIK, J.P. (1983) : *The Education Commission and After* ; Allied Publishers.
9. ——(1975) : *Policy and Performance in Indian Education 1947-74*.
10. *Ibid*, p. 20.

10 Technology and Development : A Beneficiary Oriented Approach

Padma Vasudevan,* G.S. Gujral* and Santosh*

Technology is considered to be the key to productivity. In an industrial age, it is presumed that productivity and economic returns automatically lead to development. However, somewhere in the process of industrialization, the human factor has been lost and the benefits get directed essentially to some individual or groups of persons who have the necessary capital, power and control. For example, the set of technologies useful in warfare do benefit the autocrat, but destroy large majority of people. It is now recognised that even technology package which heralded green revolution have essentially benefited the richer farmer who could afford the HYV, chemical fertilizers, pesticides and irrigation facilities. Thus it becomes imperative to pose the question : Technology for whose benefit ? Gandhiji gave the following talisman as the criterion for assessment. "Whenever you are in doubt or when the self becomes too much with you, apply the following test : Recall the face of the poorest and the weakest man whom you may have seen

* Centre for Rural Development and Appropriate Technology, I.I.T. Delhi.

and ask yourself if the step you contemplate is going to be of any use to him. Will it restore him to control over his own life and destiny. In other words, will it lead to Swaraj for the hungry and spiritually starving millions ? Then you will find your doubts and your self melting away." Einstein, one of the greatest scientists human history has known emphasised "Caring for man and his destiny must always constitute the primary interest of all technical efforts and never forget this in the midst of diagrams and equations."

Whatever, may be the ultimate touchstone accepted by the scientific community for technology assessment, it is clear that the present value system based on techno-economic criteria alone can only lead to a hightly inequitable development, widening the gap between the rich and poor. Building a future on technologies which leave a large majority of population underdeveloped is not just undesirable, but would ultimately spell disaster for the humanity as a whole. It is equally important to recognise the limits to growth in terms of resource constraints. Especially energy, materials, capital, land and water resources have to be used optimally for a sustainable future. Thus the twoba sic criteria for technology assessment have to be equitable development and ecological compatibility.

Also, it must be recognised that technology is not beneficiary neutral. Specific efforts have to be made to design appropriate technologies for the weaker sections (small and marginal farmers, artisans and women) especially in the rural areas. This section of the society is not only economically deprived but is also under-privileged due to a variety of socio-cultural constraints. For example, the organised industrial sector is not only in a position to spell out its technical problems but also has the necessary finances and organizational structures for direct interaction with the scientific community and adopting the solutions developed by R & D.

But in the case of the unorganised rural sector, the situation is quite different. While the S & T requirements have to be identified by closely working in the rural areas studying the prevailing conditions, there is hardly any incentive in the present award—reward system for the scientists to involve themselves in this manner. Generally, interaction of voluntary

agencies becomes necessary in defining the problems. Further, the financial support comes from a third type of institution, *e.g.* from the government or banking sector. Problems also arise in technology transfer. Hence coordination between various types of institutions is needed right from the stage of 'need identification' to 'technology transfer', calling for linkages as shown in Fig. 1. Specifically, it is important to know the strength and weakness of the beneficiary sector in terms of skill and resource availability as well as the socio-cultural and economic constraints so that technologies developed match with their specific requirements. This concept is illustrated by giving examples of women and small farmers as the target group.

Technologies for Women

In devising technologies for women, a number of parameters especially unique to this group has to be kept in mind. These are :

(i) the biological constraints such as child bearing and rearing ;
(ii) traditional division of labour binding them to household chores which in the case of rural women may consume as many as 16-18 hours a day ;
(iii) lack of education (they may not even be literate) ;
(iv) lack of employment and economic independence ;
(v) lack of decision-making power and a lower status in the family ;
(vi) religious and cultural bias ; and
(vii) lack of self-confidence.

Hence, the technology developed should—

(i) Reduce drudgery at home level, thereby releasing time for leisure/productive employment ;
(ii) Provide suitable remuneration which is attractive enough for the family to make the necessary adjustments ;
(iii) Be suitable for adoption at home or community level so that employment can be combined with house keeping ;

(iv) Further, suitable training needs have to be imparted at home itself or nearby, giving confidence in handling mechanical devices.

(v) Suitable systems of raw-material inputs and marketing have to be tied up with the technological infrastructure.

Technologies for Small Farmers

As in the case of women, certain unique features are also associated with the small and marginal farmers which need to be kept in view while devising technologies for them. These be listed as follows :

(i) They have small land holdings ;

(ii) Quite often the land is not fertile and proper irrigation facilities are not available ;

(iii) Lack of capital as well as risk taking capacity ;

(iv) They have to fulfil most of the basic needs from the land only ; and

(v) They face problems of post-harvest operations and storage as well as marketing.

The modern agriculture with its mechanization, high-yielding varieties (HYV), chemical fertilizers and pesticides has no answer for the problems often encountered by the small or marginal farmers. In addition to the above, the faulty agricultural practices lead to soil salinity, waterlogging or depletion of soil nutrients and water sources. Such an agriculture cannot be sustained in the long term. This calls for a rethinking on our pattern of agricultural development especially in small farms. For example, the concept of integrated utilization of land for production of not only food but also fodder, fuel, fertilizer and materials, by raising appropriate species needs to be emphasized. Further the traditional practices more compatible with environment must be evaluated again on scientific lines. Wherc feasible a technology package comprising modern and traditional practices could be introduced.

Conclusion

It is necessary that the scientific community at large should be encouraged to interact with the unorganised rural sector and analyse the problems so as to identify their S&T requirements. For this, the educational system has to be suitably reorganised with special emphasis on the following :

(i) Creating awareness among the faculty, scientists and R&D personnel about the problems of the rural sector,

(ii) Developing a technology assessment system which can analyse and help in selecting technologies for sustainable and equitable development,

(iii) Rethinking on technical issues with a futurological perspective based on a value system which considers the impact of technology not only in economic term but also in terms of equity, employment, energy, environment and socio-cultural issues.

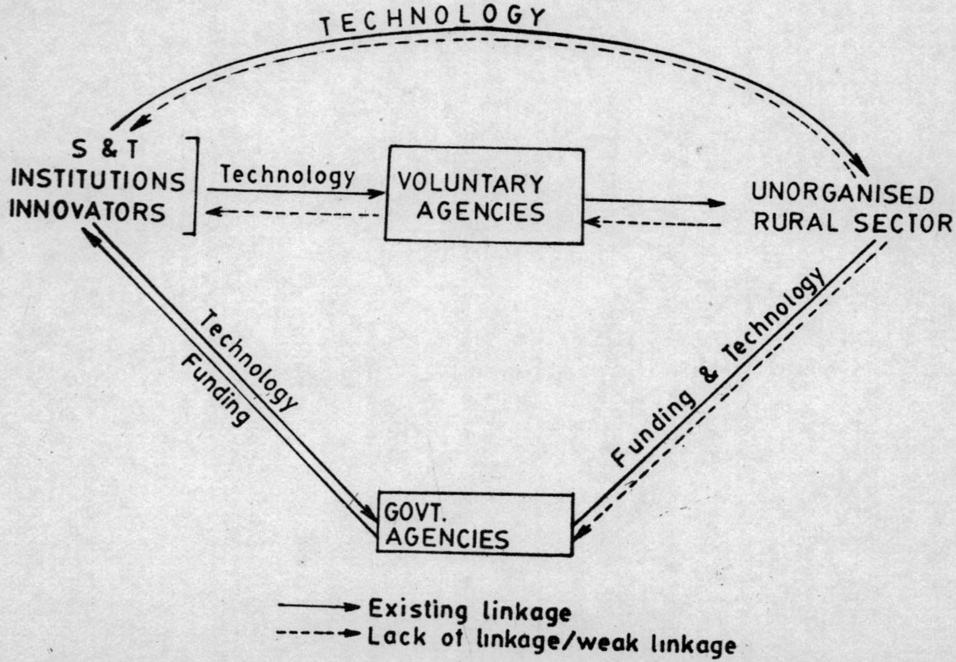
TECHNOLOGY
S & T
INSTITUTIONS
INNOVATORS
Technology
VOLUNTARY
AGENCIES
UNORGANISED
RURAL SECTOR
Technology
Funding
Funding & Technology
GOVT.
AGENCIES
Existing linkage
Lack of linkage/weak linkage

11 | Social Responsibility of Technocrats

Prof. Iqbal H. Khan* and Mrs. Majida Iqbal**

The basic philosophy of progress in our country is the dream of a socialistic pattern of society. There is general consensus upon the goals envisaged in our planning *i.e.* a rapid rise in the standard of living of the common man. It is also accepted that this rise in material prosperity can be brought about only in a technological milieu of rapid industralization and instant communication. Such a scenario will naturally put a great responsibility on the engineers for it is they, who apply their knowledge and judgement for the optimum utilization of available resources to accelerate the pace for progress and prosperity. To shoulder this immense responsibility the engineers will need to be prepared to face the challenges of future development in technology.

It is estimated that the progress made in science and technology in the 20th century is more than the progress made in the entire history of human civilization. The engineers will therefore need to keep a clear vision of the future trends in technology.

---

* Department of Civil Engineering, Jamia Millia Islamia, New Delhi.
** Research Scholar, University of Roorkee, Roorkee (U.P.)

In today's fast moving technological flux it is dangerous to make any prediction for the future. Nevertheless certain trends can be safely identified.

First the world is rapidly shrinking. More and more people will be travelling utilizing faster, safer and better systems. This will usher in an era of novel and bold technologies *e.g.* superfast trains, supersonic jet, water transport system, traffic system organisation *etc.*

Computers, telecommunication, satellite and remote sensing techniques and a wide array of information technology will be commonly available.

The teaching and learning methodologies will also undergo major changes both in outlook as well as in implementation. Today students spend a lot of their valuable time in rote learn- and cramming raw data in their minds. The difference between information knowledge and wisdom is not appreciated by the educationists. With the advent of computers and easy access to information technology there will be less need for cramming and more time and effort will be spent on thinking and analysing.

Faster communication and information systems will become a powerful vehicle for transmission of ideas and for interaction among people in distant place. In the words of Arther Clarke "ours has become the last century of the savage. For all mankind, the stone age is over".

In several fields *e.g.* agriculture, chemical engineering, biotechnology new research findings will usher an era of unprecedented progress and prosperity. Mankind will no longer suffer pangs of hunger nor the scourge of deprivation. Green revolution, wonder drugs and general abundance of material goods will benefit everybody and not just the elite. In short in each and every area of human endeavour technological progress will bring in far reaching developments.

But this will also add to the responsibilities of the technocrats and managers. In such a technological milieu it will be essential that all system work in perfect harmony. The penalty for any inefficiency and incompetence will be severe and the breakdown of any system will wreak untold misery on

the people. The recent Bhopal tragedy is a powerful reminder to the technocrats and the managers that human attitudes will need to be upgraded corresponding to the progress in Science and Technology. Even in the developed countries *e.g.* USSR, U.S.A. similar accidents happen with a disturbing frequency. The irony is that many of these accidents go unreported and thus opportunity for learning valuable lessons and building a data bank on case histories is lost.

One cannot ignore the danger to ecology and the environment due to lack of industrial discipline. It is common knowledge that the pollution in the big cities has reached alarming levels. There is little control on the quality of industrial effluents discharged in our water systems or on the quality of motor vehicle exhausts polluting the environment. Even in such routine activities as road building, construction, telephone system, power and water supply *etc.* this quality control is conspicuous by its absence. Little sensitivity is shown in such important activities as felling of trees, mining, construction of dams, location of industries, fire safety, traffic flow *etc.*

The general apathy to such macro-level problems leads one to the depressing conclusion that the state of affairs will become much worse before it becomes better.

Reckless consumption of petroleum products and industrial pollution has resulted in what is called 'The Green House Effect.' Scientists believe that it is leading to a general rise in the earth's temperature. It is estimated that the temperature has already risen by about 2°C. Such a trend will eventually bring in its wake melting of polar caps and increase in the water levels. Many coastal cities and even some entire countries (*e.g.* Maldives) are in danger of being completely wiped out by the floods feared on this account. The protective ozone layer in our atmosphere has also suffered and holes as big in size as the continent of Antarctica have appeared in this layer. It is well known that this layer protects the inhabitants of the earth by filtering out harmful radiations from the sun (*e.g.* ultra violet rays). The depletion of this layer will bring in its wake a chain of diseases and disasters to the inhabitants of the earth.

In the technologically advanced countries a number of voluntary and official agencies are working for the protection of environment. Consumer protection agencies also operate to ensure quality control. The increase in the volume of litigation and importance of legal profession in the U.S.A. today is an index of the awareness of the people to their rights of quality control and proper maintenance of all services *e.g.* telephone, and power supply. Public awareness of such issues is bound to increase in India also. One can safely conclude that all developing countries will pass through the same cycle of euphoria and depression as is witnessed in advanced countries in their technological progress.

Developing countries often borrow technology from developed countries without realising that much of the developed countries' discipline and attitudes are often built into the technology. It is essential that alongwith the machinery, the related work culture and organisation is also transplanted for the optimum operation of the particular machinery.

Environmental protection ensuring ecological balance, quality control and proper maintenance of services are some of the most urgent issues that need to be clearly understood and analysed by the engineers and technocrats.

To this end there are two essential requirements. Firstly the engineers will need to be experts in handling the sophisticated machinery and equipment. Secondly they will also need to develop leadership qualities to efficiently run huge engineering projects that will continue to proliferate in the course of development.

The first requirement is basically a question of ensuring high standards in the education of engineers. Good faculty, good laboratories and an atmosphere conducive to the academic excellence are vital components in this regard. Despite the various socio-economic constraints there is no dearth of brilliant students who come out of the engineering institutions regularly. Unfortunately there is a general weakness in the 'hands-on' experience of our students. There is a lack of motivation in acquiring, expertise in the 'nuts and bolts' aspect of the project and too much importance is given to theoretically ideal situations.

Another drawback is the lack of interest in continuing the education during their employment. A decade of experience is often one year's experience repeated ten times. Most field engineers do not care much to update and broaden their skills and expertise. This attitude is fatal in the fast moving technological milieu of today. Studies in Japan conducted by leading industrial giants *e.g.* Mitsubishi reveal that most technology of sophisticated nature becomes obsolete within five years' time. It is the responsibility of technocrats, therefore to keep themselves and their subordinates abreast with the latest developments in this field. This can be done through regular programmes of continuing education and active participation in various activities of research and development.

The second requirement *i.e.* the personal qualities of leadership is becoming more and more relevant in this climate of rapidly changing technology. Leadership does not refer to any single dimension of personality. Rather it is the term that encompasses a whole range of attributes conveying a sense of responsibility and capacity for shouldering it. Problems often arise that do not have any precedent. One cannot fall back on any text book solution or any store of past experience. Engineers will need to innovate and display creativity in crisis management. Creativity can be inculcated and the atmosphere prevailing at work place has significant correlation with the creativity of the people. Brainstorming is a technique often employed to tap the creative potential of the people.

In large complex projects it is essential that people work as a team. The days of lone heroes and indispensable autocrats are over. An engineer today has to work in harmony with his peers, his superiors and his subordinates. This democratization of work culture puts a heavy responsibility on engineers and managers to ensure regular training, updating of skills and career management of the staff engaged in a project.

Leadership qualities coupled with technical competence are a potent prescription for engineers and managers shouldering the heavy responsibility of socio-economic development of the country.

Another drawback is the lack of interest in continuing the education during their employment. A decade of experience is often one year's experience repeated ten times. Most field engineers do not care much to update and broaden their skills and expertise. This attitude is fatal in the fast moving technological milieu of today. Studies in Japan conducted by leading industrial giants e.g. Mitsubishi reveal that most technology of sophisticated nature becomes obsolete within five years' time. It is the responsibility of technocrats, therefore to keep themselves and their subordinates abreast with the latest developments in this field. This can be done through regular programmes of continuing education and active participation in various activities of research and development.

The second requirement i.e. the personal qualities of leadership is becoming more and more relevant in this climate of rapidly changing technology. Leadership does not refer to any single dimension of personality. Rather it is the term that encompasses a whole range of attributes conveying a sense of responsibility and capacity for shouldering it. Problems often arise that do not have any precedent. One cannot fall back on any text book solution or any store of past experience. Engineers will need to innovate and display creativity in crisis management. Creativity can be inculcated and the atmosphere prevailing at work place has significant correlation with the creativity of the people. Brainstorming is a technique often employed to tap the creative potential of the people.

In large complex projects it is essential that people work as a team. The days of lone heroes and indispensable autocrats are over. An engineer today has to work in harmony with his peers, his superiors and his subordinates. This democratization of work culture puts a heavy responsibility on engineers and managers to ensure regular training, updating of skills and career management of the staff engaged in a project.

Leadership qualities coupled with technical competence are a potent prescription for engineers and managers shouldering the heavy responsibility of socio-economic development of the country.

Part II
Micro Perspective

12 Economic and Political Dimensions of Pollution Need for Political Action for Environment Protection

E. Haribabu*

It is now realized that unbridled onslaught on nature will ultimately lead to the destruction of mankind. Pollution from various sources—industrial effluents and emissions, automobile exhausts and nuclear radiation—affect quality of air, water and soil in the environment. Industrial effluents released into rivers and streams affect people who live downstream and animals that depend on the rivers and streams. Industrial and auto-emissions pollute the air we breathe in. It is a situation in which benefits accrue to some people who generate pollution and costs are borne by those who use polluted water and breathe in polluted air. This is an unjust situation in which a few people gain by polluting the environment while many people stand to lose. This calls for intervention.

The question of pollution control is not merely a technical

*Department of Humanities and Social Sciences, IIT, Kanpur. The author is thankful to Dr. B.N. Patnaik for his comments on an earlier draft of the paper.

one. Technologies operate in a social context characterised by conflicting interests. Attempts to control pollution in essence are attempts to control technologies. Before we attempt to control technologies and pollution generated by technologies we should grasp inter-connections among economy, politics, and the state. An analysis of interconnections brings out the interplay of conflicting interests and values or ideologies associated with these interests. In this context, responsibilities of scientists and technologists cannot remain confined to acts of suggesting technical solutions to control pollution. Actions based on certain values are needed.

Economic Classes and Pollution

In all societies that have been using modern technology environmental pollution has become an integral feature. In a capitalist society, if an industrialist could [illegible] profits by polluting the environment he would do so. This may be too deterministic a statement but this is the reality. The reason why industrialists can pollute environment and also make maximum profits lies in the political power that the industrialists wield. Political power of the owners of industry flows from their economic power. Industrialists as a class can exercise enormous potitical power at various levels and in various ways. They can influence : (a) state policies to see that the policies further their interests ; and (b) the state agencies, regulating bodies and institutions in charge of implementing the policies especially when the regulating bodies and institutions are given discretionary power in interpreting the policies and making judgements. Further, industrialists may resort to direct and indirect threats to government. Threats, such as closure of industrial plants and retrenchment of workers, which will lead to unemployment, loss of tax revenue to the exchequer and retarding economic growth, are sufficient for a government either to ignore the problem or to pay lip service to it. Being economically powerful, the industrialists may hire the services of obliging technical experts and unleash a campaign couched in a pseudo-scientific language to convince the public and the government that pollution generated by the industry is within "accepted limits". We will examine the

problem of setting "acceptable limits" later. There are a variety of ways in which the industrial owners can dodge. They may install pollution-control equipment but may not operate it to save costs of running the equipment or they may operate it only when the inspecting authorities visit the

It should be realized that though the industrialists gain by polluting the environment in the short-run, they will lose in the long-run. Installing pollution-control equipment may increase initial costs but it pays in the long-run. Clean environment increases the productivity of the workers. However, it is difficult to convince the owners of the industry through a moral campaign. The problem has to be tackled at the poli-cal level.

State Apparatus and Pollution Control

In modern socities state intervenes to various degrees in economic, social and other spheres through its policies—industrial policies science and technology policies etc. These policies are not value-free or politically neutral. The policies reflect the values or ideology of the decision-making elite—political leadership, industrial interests and bureaucracy. Scientists and technologists are involved in formulation of policies as technical experts by the decision-makers. Experience has shown that in most of the democratic countries, policies tend to favour economically and politically powerful groups. There is a need to formulate alternative policies which do not enrich the rich and political power of the powerful. Such alternative policies would have to be based on values that promote equity and protect environm e

Responsibilities of Scientists and Technolo

In a situation where a few people gain at the cost of others by polluting the environment, protecting the environment in essence is safeguarding the interests of the majority. Today, in most of the countries a majority of the scientists and technologists do not seem to question the pollution-generating technologies and the policies that either directly or indirectly encourage such technologies. What they do is to advocate

more technology to solve the problem. Reluctance on the part of the scientists and the technologists to raise fundamental questions regarding the existing state of affairs arises from : (a) the legacy of a specific scientific tradition to which they are heirs ; and (b) their self-interests.

Scientists and technologists in today's world are heirs to a specific scientific tradition that emerged in the 17th century. This tradition is reflected in the views of the advocates of science in the 17th century. Consider the views of the founders of the Royal Society of London. In the context of religious conflicts and political uncertainties the founders of the Royal Society made a strategic compromise. The compromise was that the advocates and practitioners of science would restrict themselves to "morally neutral" study of nature and that they would not extend their scientific method to study issues related to economy and politics.[1] The compromise which was evolved as a strategy later became a virtue. It helped the scientists on the one hand and the ruling classes on the other. The ruling classes extended patronage to science and the scientists on the condition that the scientists would pursue "morally neutral" study of nature and provide utilitarian knowledge.

It is this specific tradition which has led to the depoliticization of scientists and technologists. Today, the ruling elite everywhere continuously evolve mechanisms to keep the scientists and the technologists depoliticized. In almost all societies today the state has acquired enormous control over science and the scientific institutions (financial controls, directing the scientific and technological institutions to pursue certain kind of research). In this context an individual scientist can pursue his self-interest (career advancement, funds for research, positions in the government bodies *etc.*) only by accepting the state policies and values associated with the policies. Similarly the scientists and technologists employed by the private entrepreneurs have to accept the policies of the enterprise for realizing their self-interests. Dissenting scientists and technologists are silenced in various ways: through reward, punishment, and coopting *etc.*

At another level there are problems regarding norms of

"acceptable limits" of pollution. Standards chosen by scientists to prescribe norms of "acceptable limits" of pollution or "acceptable levels of risk" can never be purely scientific. The recent controversy regarding the import of 3,000 tonnes of contaminated Irish butter by our government reveals that: (a) the standards set by scientists for deciding acceptable level of contamination differ (this is reflected by the difference of opinion between the two Nobel laureates and the Indian scientific experts appointed to examine the butter); and (b) the standards are not purely scientific.

What should Scientists and Technologists do ?

Actions intended to protect the environment and pollution control would have to be based on certain values. In so far as protection of environment and pollution control amount to safeguarding the interests of the poor, values of equity and environmental values[2] would have to be espoused by scientists and technologists. In so far as the question of equity is a political one, it calls for political participation of the scientists and technologists. Political participation is not merely exercising one's franchise at regular intervals. It calls for sustained campaign to influence the state policies and to pressurize the industrial interests to minimize pollution in the short-run and to eliminate pollution generating technologies in the long-run. In the campaign to achieve these goals scientists and technologists should systematically mobilize the poor and the powerless who are the worst affected.

Conclusion

We have thus seen that the question of environmental protection is not merely a technical matter. In this context, it is imperative that scientists and technologists must make a moral choice—whether to share the values of the rich and powerful or to espouse the values conducive for pollution-free environment and development of the poor and the powerless. In today's world a moral choice is a political choice.

REFERENCES

1. BEN-DAVID, J. (1971) : *The Scientist's Role in the Society : A Comparative Study*, New Jersey; Prentice-Hall, Englewood Cliffs, see also, Purver, M. *The Royal Society : Concept and Creation*, Massachusetts : The MIT Press, 1967.
2. BARBOUR, I.G. (1980) : *Technology, Environment and Human Values*, New York ; Praeger Publishers, Ch. 5, see also Agassi J. *Technology : Philosophical and Social Aspects*, Dordrecht ; D. Reidel Publishing Company, 1985.

13 Communication Responsibility of Social Scientists and Managers : The Case of Psychology and Advertising

Lila Krishnan*

One of the many responsibilities that scientists, technologists and managers have towards society is that of communicating information that will further the interests and welfare of society. In this context the present paper aims at highlighting certain issues pertaining to communication by psychologists as social scientists, and by sales managers through advertising. Although many of the comments made here may apply to other social scientists, and specialists in other areas, the focus will be on psychologists as researchers and sales managers as advertisers. Most of the issues raised here are debatable and there will be supporters for both the pro and con views. The i ea is to focus attention to these issues because they do not em to be taken seriously in the fields of psychology and advertisement.

*Department of Humanities & Social Sciences, IIT, Kanpur (U.P.).

Three features that are common to research psychologists and advertisers are, first, that both deal with aspects of behaviour, secondly, that both are interested in publicizing their wares, and thirdly, that both are responsible for communicating information to the community of human beings who are both the subject and object of their respective professions. Both psychologists and advertisers provide information that creates and changes public attitudes and behaviour ; psychologists publish their research findings which have implications for behaviour, and advertisers provide information about products that they want consumers to buy. The main question being considered here is : how can the psychologists and the advertiser optimally fulfil their responsibility of communicating information, in view of certain dilemmas that the two must inevitably face ?

These dilemmas may now be examined.

The first dilemma arises out of the incompatibility often found between the *professional* responsibility of the psychologist and sales manager, on the hand, and their *ethical* res-responsibility, on the other. The psychologist, like other scientists, is expected to keep the scientific community, and ultimately the public at large, well-informed about his research findings. This means that the research findings have to be reported as honestly and as completely as possible However, does this mean that all findings must be reported, regardless of their positive or negative consequences ? Similarly, in the case of the sales manager, on one hand, there is an expectation that he should maximize sales in keeping with the goals of the organization for which he is working. On the other hand, he may be aware of the negative aspects of the product he is expected to sell. Should the manager advertise all the products he wishes to sell, regardless of their positive or negative consequences for the consumer ?

This question can be answered in more than one way, of course. There will be those who believe that the psychologist and the advertiser must fulfil their professional responsibility of providing honest, complete information—"the truth, the whole truth, and nothing but the truth"—including both

positive and negative consequences of the information they are communicating. In other words, both the psychologist and the manager would be fulfilling their professional responsibility of conveying information and indicating that such information could be "ambipotent for good or evil", in the words of Lowrance (1985, p. 16). The receiver of the information has a responsibility, too, and it is the receiver who should then decide how he would use the information. This view is reminiscent of what Edward Teller, the father of the hydrogen bomb, had to say with respect to the responsibility of scientists for destructive weapons.

"...I...believe that we would be unfaithful to the tradition of Western civilization if we were to shy away from exploring the limits of human achievements. It is our specific duty as scientists to explore and to explain. Beyond that our responsibilities cannot be any greater than those of any other citizen of our democratic society...I am confident that, whatever the scientists are able to discover or invent, the people will be good enough . . . to control it for the ultimate benefit of everyone." (In Weinberg, 1959, p. 75).

In other words, according to the view just presented, it is a scientist's responsibility merely to tell the world all about his research findings. Utilization of this information is not his responsibility. In the case of advertising managers, perhaps this is the only view that can be taken because there is an economic motive behind their endeavour. All the products made by their company must be advertised and sold ; or else, those products should not be made at all. The psychologist is fortunately in a better position to made a judgement and choice.

There are also those who disagree with the view expressed above, and do not believe that the scientist is absolved of the responsibility of how is research findings are utilized. Bertrand Russell (1960) voices the opinion of this camp :

> The scientist is also a citizen : and citizens who have any special skill have a public duty to see, as far as can, that their skill is utilized in accordance with the public interest ... It is impossible in the modern world for a man of science to say with any honesty, 'My business is to provide

knowledge, and what use is made of the knowledge is not my responsibility," (p. 391).

The implication is that if a scientist is aware of the harmful consequences of communicating a particular piece of information, it may be necessary for him to think twice about communicating it at all. It has already been clarified that this view may not practically apply to the advertiser ; for the psychologist it means asking the question : does communicating a particular bit of information significantly modify the existing body of knowledge in the area, or provide useful applications ? Does such a communication have harmful consequences ? If so, can these harmful consequences be justified on the basis of furthering scientific knowledge and/or improving human life ?

An example from psychology will serve to clarify these questions. The famous controversy regarding the genetic basis of IQ differences between races (Jensen, 1969) led to furious debates with protests against the way in which empirical evidence was interpreted. The issue raised here is this : even if it is true that the genetic basis is stronger in racial differences components in IQ than environmental differences, how does this help the world community (except perhaps 'explain' the perceived superiority of some races, usually white) ? Emphasizing genetic components in anything is tantamount to admitting that nothing can be done to change the situation. The negative consequences of such information can be quite severe and long-lasting. If it is 'known' that some races are 'genetically inferior' in intelligence to others, a perpetual prejudice against members of such races is almost assured—with the enthusiastic support of the expert scientific community. Fortunately, although such prejudices still exist, the situation could be much worse. Such examples should serve to make psychologists and other social scientists more cautious in reporting their research findings.

The second dilemma is also essentially a moral one and is related to the first one. Do the psychologist and advertiser have the right to communicate information that creates or changes attitudes and behaviour, and thereby creates specific values ?

Once again, this question may be answered in the affirmative by some, and in the negative by others.

On the one hand it may be considered inevitable that values will be created through scientific endeavours, that..."Science and technology affect our philosophies and choices by : deeply informing our cultural outlook ; creating opinions for public consideration ...and inducing value changes..." (Lowrance, 1985, p. 16). In such a case it is assumed that nothing can be done because it is impossible to think of a value-free science. Moreover, the responsibility of holding a set of beliefs or values rates also with recipients of information, continuing the same argument that was made in the context of the first question.

On the other hand, one might say that the psychologist and advertiser do not have a right to communicate information if it creates a particular value because of the way in which the information is presented. As was seen in the example given above, communicating a specific bit of scientific evidence—however honestly reported—might have more harmful than useful consequences. Judging 'harmful' or 'useful' consequences itself involves values, undoubtedly. But the communicator should still be watchful about subtly introducing labels of 'good' or 'bad' on the information he presents, about conveying opinions as though they were facts, or about reporting incomplete information that may create biases.

To cite an example from psychology, it is believed by some that having an 'extroverted' personality is better than being introverted, or that being 'modern' is better than being 'traditional'. Although information regarding these qualities might actually have been presented quite neutrally at the source, biases may be introduced quite subtly. Thus the researcher may report a high positive correlation between being extroverted and being mentally healthy, or between being modern and qualities such as being more efficient, well-read, and believing that one can control one's own destiny—all of which are highly valued at least in urban societies. Right away, a value has been created.

In the same view, an example can be given of research findings that have a potential for creating specific biased beliefs because of their contradictory or ambiguous nature. Examining

the relationship between stress and peptic ulcers, Brady (1958) reported the following experiment on 'executive monkeys' and its results. Two monkeys were fixed to an apparatus and were given mild but unpleasant electric shocks intermittently. The onset of the shocks was unpredictable. One of the monkeys was provided with a switch that would turn off the shock ; the other monkey had no such mechanism, and could do nothing when the shocks came. It was found that after some time, the monkey that could turn off the shocks developed peptic ulcer. This was explained on the basis of stress created by the constant anxiety to switch off the shock. The stress was due to perceived control over the shocks. Some years later, Weiss (1972) reported just the opposite findings with rats : the rat that was unable to switch off the shocks was the one which developed ulcer. The inference was that perceived uncontrollability of unpleasant events created stress.

A researcher who wishes to substantiate the hypothesis that perceived control creates stress would cite only Brady's finding : one who wishes to prove the opposite would cite only Weiss's finding. If a researcher is aware of both sets of findings, then it is ethically improper for him to communicate only one side of the story because this might generate biased beliefs regarding perceiving control/a lack of control over unpleasant events.

In the area of advertising, biased communication in this sense appears to be the rule rather than the exception—for obvious reasons. Advertising has become synonymous with a change of attitudes towards specific products which in turn modifies and determines buying behaviour. Much has been written about how the advertising world has led to consumerism. Legislative measures against misleading information ('The Consumer Boom', *India Today*, Feb. 1984) about food products helps in reducing such advertising (including ready foods and drinks that contain chemicals which can be harmful in the long run). However, it is difficult to enact legislation for advertising that creates values by playing upon specific human motives. For example, displaying suiting material (or even brands of tea or coffee) that go with 'being sophisticated', or cosmetics that are said to beautify because of

special ingredient, accomplishes good sales and, at the same time, makes the consumer responsible for his own gullibility. It is extremely rare to find an advertisement that presents both the good and bad points of the product : an exception is cigarette advertisements which, while claiming all sorts of pleasant experiences, also insert the 'statutory warning' that cigarette smoking can be injurious to health—a case of presenting both sides of the information.

In short, there is no doubt that the advertising world is not particularly concerned about the values created. Yet, as mentioned earlier, because of their professional responsibilities, this issue of creating values has to be looked at in a different perspective for advertisers than for psychologists as scientists.

Having posed the dilemmas of communicating information faced by psychologists and advertisers, suggestions regarding the resolution of these dilemmas are in order. As in the case of all moral questions it would be awkward to provide definite and one-sided answers to the questions mentioned above. However, suggestions can certainly be made in an attempt to make these questions more salient to psychologists (and social scientists in general) and advertisers (and managers in general). The three suggestions below are being made in order to draw attention to the dilemmas posed earlier.

1. It is suggested that the psychologist should continue to be free to pursue research on any topic of interest to him (barring those that have serious negative implications). But he should also be urged to consider carefully the consequences of communicating information about his research findings. He should then reserve the right to publicize or not to publicize information that has more harmful than useful consequences. Part of his problem is that of lagging behind in the publishing race if he does not unconditionally submit his work for publication : it should simply be remembered that publishing is also part of today's so-called academic values. Similarly, the advertiser should also, as far as possible, make a judgment regarding communication of information regarding products that

are potentially harmful. It is acknowledged that this task may be practically more difficult for the advertiser.

2. At least the psychologist as a social scientist can be encouraged to make a choice regarding the kind of medium (mass or specialized) through which he presents his information. Depending on the topic he may decide on the mass media and a 'lighter' presentation : for more rigorous reporting he may choose journals meant mainly for experts in the field. The form of communication may then be appropriately chosen. Moreover, journals would do well to accept or reject information submitted for publication, not merely on the basis of scientific value, but also on the basis of human value (once again, a value!). So far emphasis has been laid on the ethical code of conduct of psychological research ; now, some attention should also be paid to the ethical code of *communication* of information.

   Because it is the advertiser's job to publicize his wares through whatever media are available, this suggestion would clearly not apply to advertisers.

3. If the shaping of values and changing of public attitudes and behaviour cannot be avoided by the psychologist and advertiser, than at least attempts should be made to caution the recipients of the communicated information regarding the various aspects of the content on one hand, and the overall gullibility or persuaibility of the recipients, on the other. Essentially this means that the receivers of such communication must be educated. Although such an exercise has been attempted in the area of advertising in some parts of the world, by way of consumer awareness programme and consumer-protective slogans, a parallel exercise does not seem to have been carried out in the area of psychological research. Very few lay persons know how to interpret scientific psychological research evidence.

It is hoped that there will be a growing awareness among

psychologists and advertisers, social scientists and managers, that they do have the responsibility of communicating information to the world in the way most appropriate for benefiting humanity. For any human endeavour can be considered suicidal if it does not consider human welfare as its topmost priority.

REFERENCES

BRADY, J.V. (1958) : "Ulcers in executive monkeys. *Scientific American, 199*, 95.

India Today (1984) : "The Consumer Boom".

JENSEN, A.R. (1969) : "How much can we boost IQ and scholastic achievement? *Harvard Educational Review, 39*, 1-123.

LOWRANCE, W.W. (1985); "*Modern Science and Human Values*". Oxford University Press.

RUSSELL, B. (1960) : "The social responsibilities of scientists". *Science, 131*, 391-392.

WEINBERG, M. (Ed.) (1959) : "*Issues in Social Science*", Englewood—Cliffs, N.J. : Prentice-Hall.

WEISS, J.M. (1972) : "Psychological factors in stress and disease". *Scientific American, 226*, 106.

14 | Social Implications of Waste Management

Dr. Sushil*

Introduction

Waste Management (WM) is a dynamically emerging field with vaste scope. The growing urbanization and industrialization is making WM a complex problem with serious sociological, ecological and economic implications. A sustained effort is needed to restore the socio-ecological balance of nature in order to optimally harness the available resources.

This paper emphasizes to deal with the problem of waste in totality considering its technical as well as social aspects and highlighting the social implications of effective WM. A sort of social cost-benefit analysis should be done prior to the implementation of any WM programme. It has been emphasized that in the socio-economic resource structure of India, Management of waste plays an important role.

* Centre for Management Studies, I.I.T., Delhi

Waste Management : An Overview

From system's view point, waste has been visualized as any unnecessary input to or any undesirable output from any system encompassing all types of resources, *viz.*, manpower, material energy, space, time, capital, utilities and services, data and information *etc.* The resource based classification of waste is shown in Figure 1. Waste Management (WM) is conceptualized as a multidisciplinary activity to minimise the overall wastivity of the system under consideration (1,2,5). A systematic approach to WM encompassing the waste of all kinds of resources at all stages should be adopted. However, as the material constitutes a major faction of the total product cost, material wastes are of critical importance.

Complementarity of Waste Management and Resource Management

A system basically takes some input, process it and gives the desired output, as shown in Figure 2 *i.e.*, some input is essential, in whatever form, for the functioning of a system. An ideal system is conceptualized to transform the total input into useful or desirable output. In view of the known physical laws of nature the existence of an ideal system is not possible, *i.e.* 100 per cent utilization of resources is not practically possible for any system. To paraphrase, some waste is inevitable in the functioning of any system.

The main objective of WM is to minimize the waste this aiming at the ideal system, while the resource management aims to maximise the utilization of the resources. The goal of waste and resource management is same, *i.e.*, optimal utilization of the available resources for higher efficiency and growth of the system, but the approaches are different. The relationship of waste and resource management is shown in Figure 3. It can be said that waste and resource management are complementary to each other. If one is primal formulation of a problem, the other is dual.

Concept of Wastivity

An ideal or perfect system will be one that consumes just the right amount of resources, leaving no idle, unutilized

(nonrecoverable) or lost resource, or any undesirable output. The concept of "wastivity" which is yet in the rudimentary stages may prove to be a good measure of performance, both at macro and micro levels, and will be helpful in the sound planning and monitoring of various systems at different levels of hierarchy.

"Wastivity of any system is defined as the ratio of the waste to the input".[2]

$$\text{Wastivity} = \frac{\text{Waste}}{\text{Input}}$$

Depending upon the level of waste under consideration the wastivity may be categorised as gross wastivity and net wastivity. The wastivity for each type of input indirectly assesses the productivity of each type of input. Both productivity and wastivity are complementary to each other, which bears in it the inherent cause-effect phenomenon. If the cause, *i.e.* wastivity is checked, the effect, i.e. productivity, will automatically be improved.

The Functional Elements of Waste Management

The problems associated with the management of waste in today's society are complex and diverse in nature. For an effective and orderly management of wastes the fundamental aspects and relationships must be identified and clearly understood. The efficient WM comprises the guide identification of waste generated/caused, economic reduction, efficient collection and handling, optimal sense and recycling, and effective disposal of waste leaving no environmental problems. WM can thus be functionally classified into five basic elements, *viz.*, generation, reduction collection, recycling and disposal. However, Waste Management (WM) should be viewed in totality considering the inter-relationship of basic functional elements/systems as shown in Figure 4. One of the objectives of WM is to optimise these basic functional systems to provide the most efficient and economic solution, commensurate with the constraints imposed.

By considering each element separately it is possible to :

(i) identify the fundamental aspects and relationships involved in each element :

(ii) develop, wherever possible, quantifiable relationships for the purpose of making engineering comparisons, analysis and evaluation.

Socio-economic Benefits of Waste Management Programmes

Some of the social and economic benefits of effective WM programmes and systems are as follows :

(i) Cheaper products due to increased productivity.
(ii) Reduced scarcity of materials by way of material conservations.
(iii) Economic gains by salvaging waste materials.
(iv) Introduction of newer products by recycling/reusing wastes.
(v) Relief from energy crisis.
(vi) More hygienic, safe and pollution free environment.
(vii) Lesser public nuisance due to reduction in diseases.
(viii) Neat, clean and comfortable living conditions, and higher standard of living.
(ix) Reduced uncertainty, better prediction and control of of natural calamities by nature conservation.
(x) Preservation of heritage, fauna and flora.
(xi) Control over unemployment and the development of a healthier society, and.
(xii) Speedier and sustained national development and self-reliance.

Development of Economic System

Many a time growth and development of the economic system are treated as synonymous. The consumption of resources is considered a growth measure. More consumption does not necessarily mean more development. The development of the economic system is dependent upon the effectiveness of utilization of the inputs, which is very much related to the management of waste in the economy. It is advocated here that the waste parameters deserve explicit consideration in view of their important role in various systems. The need to incorporate waste as a parameter in socio-economic planning can hardly be overemphasized by taking into consideration the crisis of vita lly needed resources, balanced economic growth

of the nation, and the awareness for a cleaner and hygienic environment.[6]

The techno-economic structure has conventionally been concentrating on intermediate means and intermediate ends. The ultimate means and ultimate ends in the spectrum, as shown in Figure 5,(4) have most of the time been ignored. This has led to serious social as well as ecological problems at both the ends. In order to minimize such socio-ecological problems the base has to be widened to incorporate the ultimate means as well as the ultimate end. WM can provide answer to interlink various stages from the ultimate means to the ultimate ends in an effective manner.

The low entropy resources are being consumed exorbitantly and in the process high entropy wastes are generated. This is leading to a continuous increase of the entropy of the whole socio-economic system. This rate of growth of entropy has to be checked if the human race wants to survive for long and at a higher level of development. The entropy can be brought under control by managing the waste in the economic system effectively. The technology and WM can be taken as a substitute of negentropy, (3) as the technological progress enables the economic extraction of lower grade natural resources and improved technology and WM result in lower wastivity of the economy.

Socio-Technical System

From socio-technical system's view point every organisation is an integrated system having interacting technical and social sub-systemes as shown in Figure 6. The organisation taken both the technical and social inputs, gives the output of technical as well as social nature, and generates both the technical and the social system waste. The relationship of technical and social system waste is shown in Figure 7. The technical system's waste increase the social system's waste and *vice versa*. Waste, whether technical or social, affects the social system within the system and the environment through the links of quality, productivity and environmental pollution.

In this regard selection of technology is an important managerial consideration. A wrong choice of technology will

lead to consequent waste of resources as well as cause social problems. For example, if a capital intensive technology is selected, for a country like India with vast amount of manpower available, in a sector where it is not needed, it will result in the waste of capital, manpower and energy. Managers can play a vital role in the selection of appropriate technology.

Social Responsibilities and Interfacing Problems

It is the social responsibility of every scientist, technologist and manager to design and manage systems which are leading to minimum level of wastivity as shown in Figure 8. There are two sub-systems in the technology cycle. One is technology development system and the other is technology management system. Scientists, technologists and managers have their social responsibilities with respect to both the systems. However, the scientists and technologists have higher responsibilities for the technology development system, whereas the managers are more responsible for the technology management system.

Scientists and technologists fulfil their social responsibilities by designing and developing technologies that minimize the wastivity, and there, meet the social needs of the system and the environment in the best possible manner.

Manager's social responsibilities are also very wide, and by managing the system's waste they contribute towards better performance of social system by obviating some interfacing socio-economic problems such as resource crisis, environmental pollution, psychological and social stresses *etc.* as shown Figure 9.

Conclusion

The need and importance of WM in the socio-economic system has been emphasized and the social implications of effective WM are highlighted. It is concluded that in order to create awareness in this regard the engineering curricula should incorporate some topics on systems approach to WM and its socio-economic implications. It is hoped that, if the professionals come out of the narrow conventional approach to WM and adopt a broader systems approach to WM, it will help in the development of a better socio-economic order.

REFERENCES

1. AGRAWAL, S.K. (SUSHIL) (1980) : "Systems Approach to Waste Management in India," M. Tech. Dissertation, Department of Mechanical Engineering, I.I.T., Delhi.
2. ——(1984) : System Modelling of Wast Management in National Planning", Ph. D. Thesis, I.I.T. Delhi.
3. AYRES, R.U. (1978) : *Resources, Environment and Economics : Applications of Materials/Energy Balance Principle*, John Wiley, New York.
4. Canadian Environmental Advisory Council (1986) : "Examining Environment-Economy Linkages," Environment Canada, Ottawa, Canada.
5. ——(1985) : "Systems Approach to Waste Management", *Industrial Engg. Journal*, Vol xiv, No. 11, 19-22.
6. ——(1987) : "I-O-W Model for National Planning," *International Journal of Systems Science*, Vol. 18, No. 11, 2043-2063.

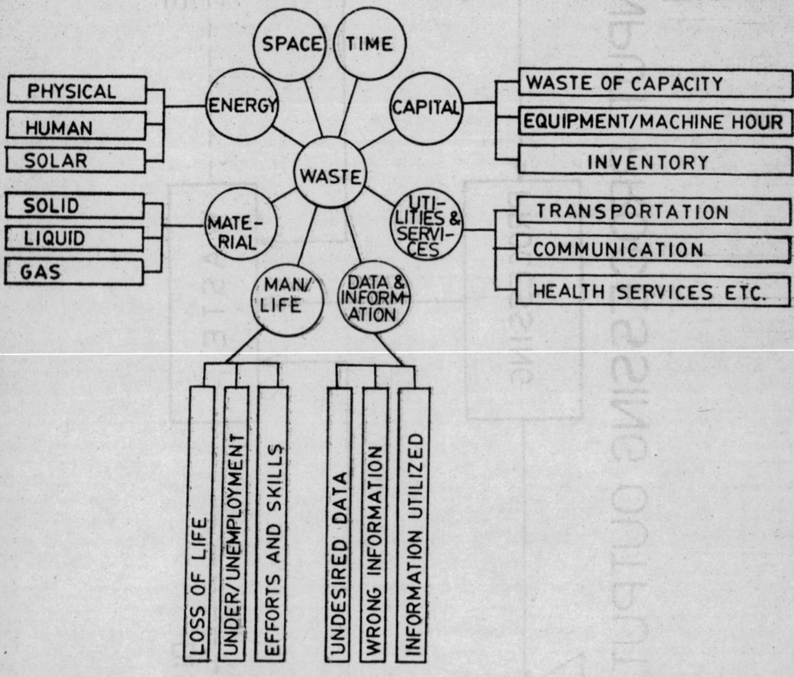

FIG.1-RESOURCE BASED CLASSIFICATION OF WASTES

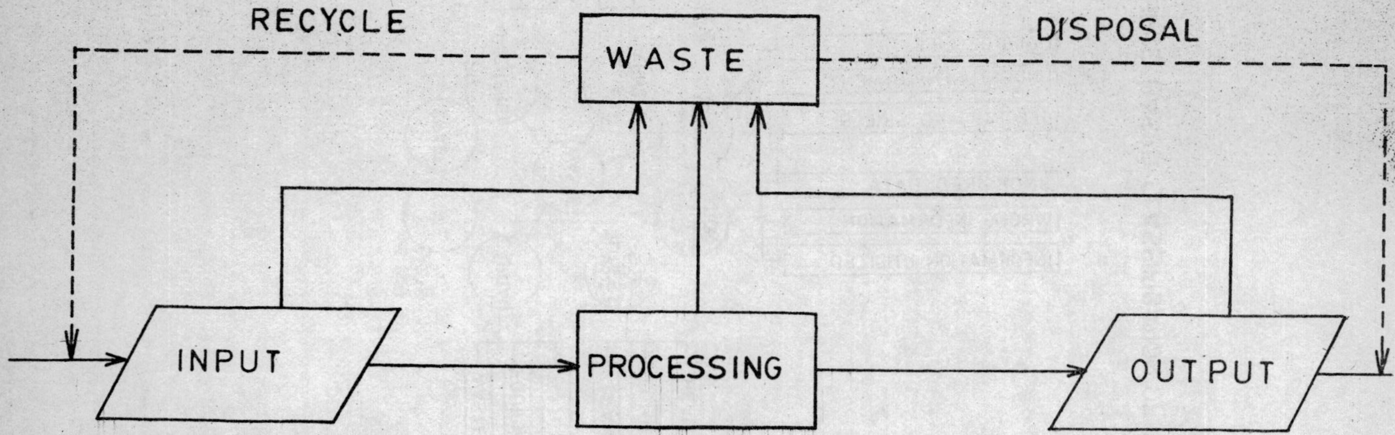

FIG. 2-INPUT PROCESSING OUTPUT SYSTEM

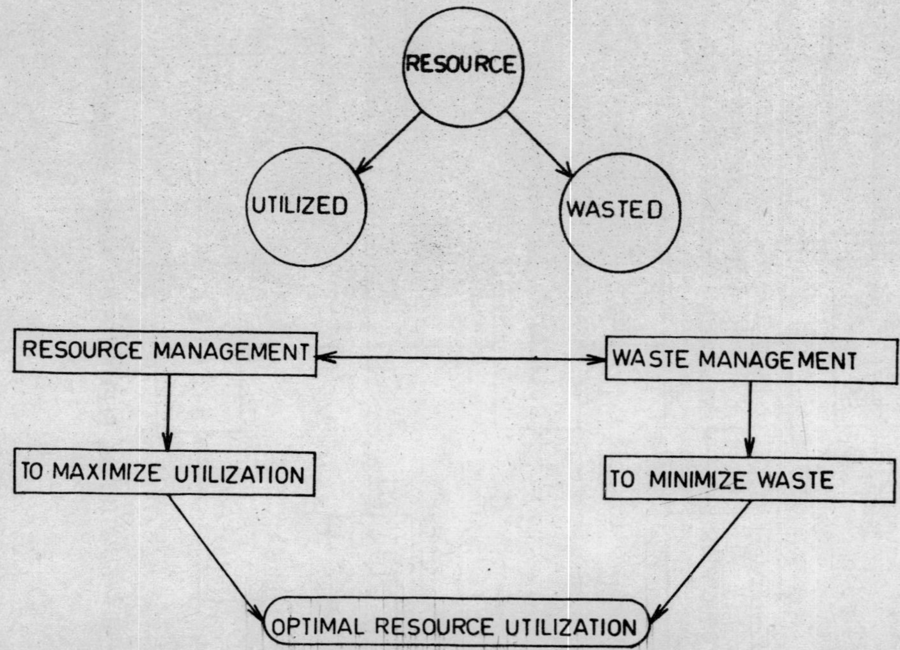

FIG. 3—COMPLEMENTARY RELATIONSHIP OF WASTE MANAGEMENT AND RESOURCE MANAGEMENT

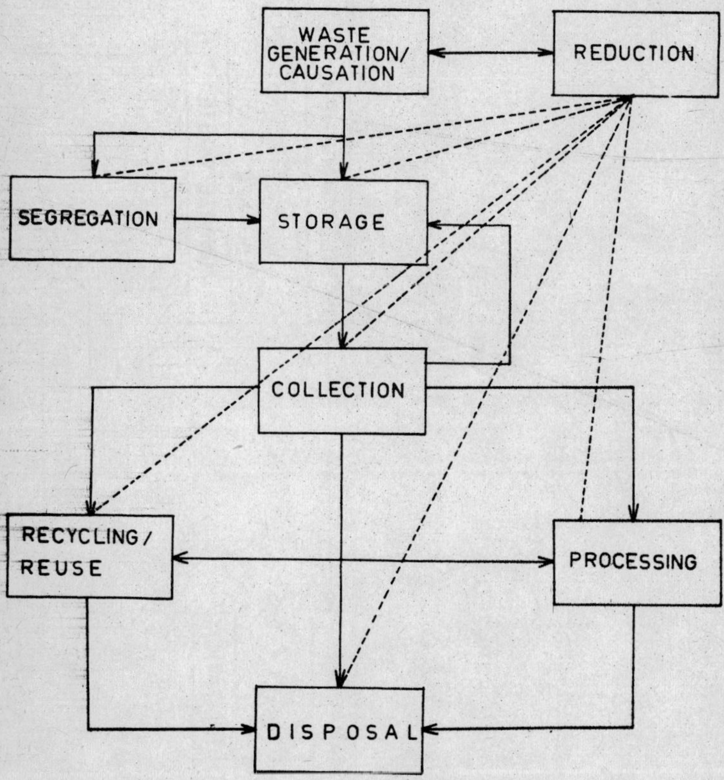

FIG. 4 - FUNCTIONAL ELEMENTS OF WASTE MANAGEMENT

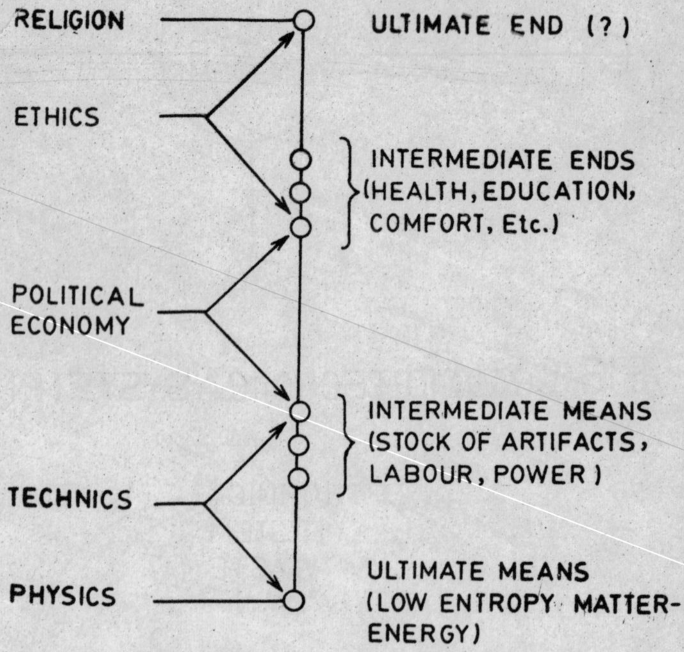

FIG. 5-SPECTRUM OF ENDS AND MEANS

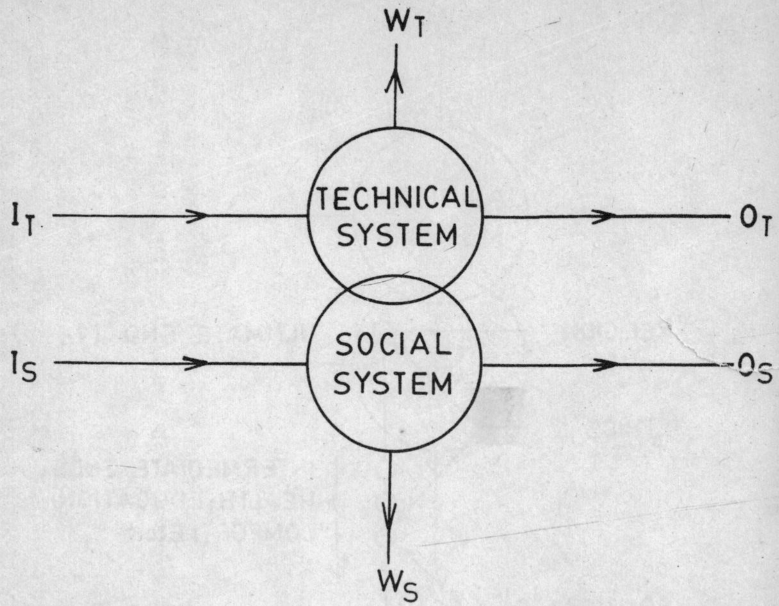

FIG. 6-SOCIO-TECHNICAL SYSTEM

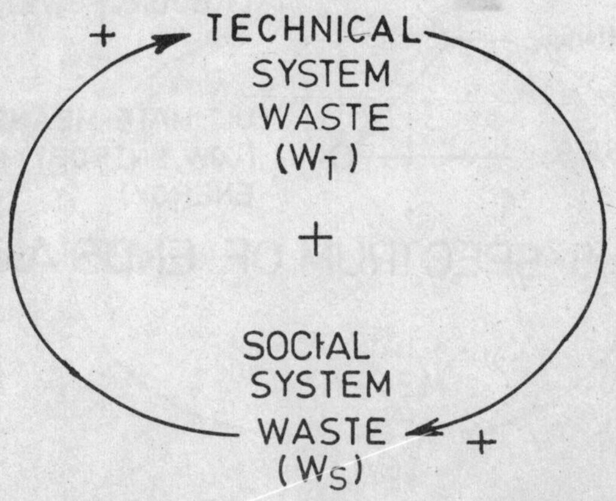

FIG.7-TECHNICAL & SOCIAL SYSTEM WASTE RELATIONSHIP

bring it in line with the WHO/UNESCO International Code of Marketing.

In India, the consumer movement, being in the stage of infancy, is not very powerful yet. There is, however, no dearth of laws enacted for the purpose of safeguarding the consumer interest. The Consumer Protection Act of 1986 is one of the important acts in this regard.

The Consumer Protection Act of 1986 sets out the rights of consumers in relation to the manufacturer and trader. A consumer can get his defective goods replaced or price refunded or secure compensation for any loss if he proves that his purchase arose out of an unfair trade practice by a trader, producer or manufacturer.

An unfair trade practice is a trade practice, which, for the purpose of promoting the sale, use or supply of any goods or for the provision of any services adopts one or more of the specified practices and thereby causes loss or injury to the consumers of such goods and services, whether by eliminating or restricting competition or otherwise.

Broadly, unfair trade practices would involve all types of misleading, false and wrong representations either in writing or orally ; sales of goods which do not comply with the standards prescribed by competent authority : all business promotion schemes announcing "bargain prices, "free gifts", "contests", "lottery" "game of chance or skill" *etc.*, involving element of deception : and manipulation of sales with a view to raising prices.

Advisory and adjudicatory forums at the district, state and national levels by the central and state governments are to be set up under this act. The progress in terms of establishment of these forums has, however, been very slow. The central government set up the Central Consumer Protection Council in June, 1987 with 150 official and non-official members. It is highly unlikely that such a big body can really play an effective role in advising the government and consumers. At the state level, the progress has been at snail's pace. Many of the bigger states have yet to set up the consumer protection council. Only a small number of states and Union territories has started the mechanism for consumer grievance redressal.

One reason why there has been such a slow progress in setting up of the redressal agencies is the paucity of funds. The Centre and the Planning Commission have been blamed for not providing adequate funds though the Act was to be implemented as a Plan Scheme. Planning Commission officials, however, argue that the decision to meet the expenditure on the redressal agencies out of the Plan Funds was only taken as an interim measure. Since consumer protection is not a developmental activity, it should be converted into a non-plan-scheme. Planners are also opposed to setting up a whole new bureaucracy to deal with the complaints of consumers. There is no need for permanent posts : the staff can be drawn from the existing departments.

As a cost-cutting measure, it has been proposed that the district forums be set up in Commissioner's divisions instead of individual districts as has been done in Rajasthan. In Rajasthan six district forums look after the work of all its 27 districts. This, however, would lead to dilution of the Act and, therefore, would defeat the very purpose of the Act which provides for a redressal forun in each district of the state. Complaints will come only when the redressal machinery is easily accessible.

There is also a problem of non-availability of judicial members to lead the councils. States are also being accused of converting the councils and forums into another channel for rewarding their loyalists by making them members, thus politicising their functioning. Similarly, as has been the case in some states, appointment of industrialists in large numbers as members in the consumer bodies which should be repr sented mainly by consumer also goes against the very spirit of the Act.

The inaction of the government in setting up the adjudicatory agencies clearly indicates lack of sincerity on the part of governments in implementing the legislation. This also indicates that the parliamentary control over the executive in regard to proper implementation of legislation is highly ineffective.

The Monopolies and Restrictive Trade Practices (MRTP) Act also provides an effective means for the redressal of the

grievances of the consumer. Initially devised to curb "monopolistic" and "restrictive trade", this act came into its own in 1984 when the addition of "unfair trade practices" through an amendment widened its scope to cover numerous categories of unfair trade practices. The MRTP Act now stands almost parallel to the Consumer Protection Act However, unlike the Consumer Protection Act, the MRTP Act excludes from its purview government departments, public secter undertakings and the co-operative sector.

The MRTP Act is implemented country-wide by the MRTP Commission with its office in Delhi. The Commission has the status of High Court and has the powers to grant injunction in cases of grave public concern.

While the Consumer Protection Act comes into operation only after an offence is committed, the MRTP Commission's job is to prevent such practices to start with. Under the Consumer Protection Act the individual must himself be an agrieved consumer seeking redressal whereas under MRTP, he need not be. The consumer or observer can just bring to the notice of the commission an unfair trade practice in operation.

The MRTP Commission has also given the consumers the power to pursue complaints on their own. A complainant is entitled to participate in the proceedings by way of producing evidence and cross examining witness of the respondent. However, in case the complainant pursued the inquiry himself he would have to bear the expenses of the same.

In the cases filed by the complainant directly, the Director General of Investigation and Registration, Department of Company Affairs, was also entitled to take part in the proceedings but not to the exclusion of the complainant until and unless the complainant ceased to pursue the inquiry. In such an eventuality, the Director General is entitled to take full charge of the proceedings.

In addition to the Consumer Protection Act and MRTP Act mentioned above, we also have specific laws for several commodity groups. Food products in India are covered by a number of Acts : The Prevention of Food Adulteration Act,

the Vegetable Oil Products Orders, the Fruit Products Orders, the Drug and Cosmetics Act, the Meat Food Products Orders and Sugar Control Orders. The main objectives of the food laws are to protect the consumer against ill-health caused by adulteration ; restrict and control, the use of food additives and to confirm the nutritional standards of the food. These laws are meant to ensure that food articles which the public buys should be prepared, packed and stored under sanitary conditions and with such ingredients and such processes so as not to be injurious to the health of people who consume it. These laws are applicable for both kinds of foods whether manufactured indigenously or imported. However, here again, the consumer is not protected effectively, a large number of laws notwithstanding. The adulteration of food items is a story which goes on repeating itself.

In case of textiles there are a number of acts and measures. One of them requires textile mills to print the composition of the fabric on the selvedge. However, the consumer has no way of testing. The more reputed manufacturers give the correct proportion with the others, the consumer takes a chance.

This brief review of regulatory environment for the protection of consumer interest shows that there is a plethora of legislation on this subject. This may create confusion. The consumer would be in a dilemma as to which agency he should approach for redressal of his grievances. What is required here is a clear-cut demarcation of areas of consumer interests in different legislations as well as proper co-ordination among different implementing agencies so as to avoid duplication of efforts.

Some consumer organizations have suggested setting up a task force to achieve better interaction between the government and various consumer forums. The task force could also act as a clearing house for the problems arising out of the implementation of the Consumer Protection Act. They have urged the government to create a special fund for the purpose of consumer protection. This fund could also be utilized for creating consumer awareness.

It has also been suggested that consumer education should

be introduced in schools and colleges as such education was vital if people were to benefit from consumer protection laws. The business community could also undertake the task o educating the consumers. Consumer education programme would provide an opportunity to the businessmen also to know the views of the consumers.

Management of business enterprises are well advised to behave in ways which will avoid drawing adverse attention to themselves from regulators and protectors of the consumer interest. Rather than taking an adverse view of the regulations, they should react positively to issues raised by consume groups.

Under the Seventh Plan a new scheme called 'Consumer Protection through Science and Technology' is being implemented. The task is to create consumer items, evolve relevant S and T input and provide action plans. It is the social responsibility of scientists and technologists to develop simpler experimental methods and test kits in order to make adultertion-testing a mass movement and facilitate continuous mon toring of quality of products. Scientists and technologists can also play an important role in providing scientific information on selected consumer items, especially the food items of mass consumption, to enable the consumers to use items safe for their health.

Lack of sincerity on the part of government in implementing the laws is one of the main reasons why these laws have failed to make an impact. Our parliament generally enacts legislations in a skeleton form and than delegates rule-making and enforcement powers to the executive. The consumer for whose benefit these laws have been enacted hardly gets any protection from these laws because of half-hearted and faulty implemention of these laws by the executive. In such a case, one recourse available to consumers is the use of courts to enforce the consumers' rights. In the US and other Western countries where the consumer movement is relatively strong, this method has proved to be quite successful. In India also the use of courts to enforce the eonsumer's rights is now widely accepted. However, the stipulated legal procedure is very expensive and long-drawn. The time-factor will be frustrating

even to the most enthusiastic consumers and voluntary organisations. It has been suggested that the total period of settlement of grievances in normal cases should not be more than a few months. To achieve that judiciary will have to adopt an activist and goal oriented approach to ensure that the acts enacted to protect the consumer are translated into action.

Conclusion

It may be stated that a vigorous consumer movement is a necessary condition for safeguarding the interests of consumer. Consumer interests cannot be protected by legislative measures alone. Unless consumers become organized and vigilant and assert their rights in a responsible manner, not much can be expected from the government enforcement machinery.

REFERENCES

The Consumer Protection Act, 1989

KUMAR, NARESH (1989) : "Consumer Protection : Operational Problems" ; *The Economic Times*, May 14.

RAO, S.L., (1988) : "Marketing and Public Policy ; "*Economic and Political Weekly*, Vol. XXIII, No. 9 Feb, 27.

16 | Industrial Accidents : Whose Responsibility ?

Raka Sharan*

Many major industrial crises and disasters are called as accidents. In reality they may not be a true accident ; they may be the result of human errors or carelessness. Can such accidents be called as accident ? The literal meaning of the word accident is "event happening by chance or Mishap" (*Oxford Dictionary*) whereas, it is well known, that many accidents, especially industrial, this take place because of sheer by design. 'Design' have been over emphasized here because certain accidents simply occur due to cumulative expansion of hazardous products. Mitroff says that one cannot prevent all accidents taking place, but one should be responsible for thinking about them. This is true that total elimination of accidents is not possible. No matter how much we try we cannot have a zero-risk society. However, some accidents can definitely be avoided by better planning and care.

This study tries to analyse the diverse perspectives of industrial accidents in the back-drop of Bhopal gas accident.

---

* Department of Humanities and Social Sciences, IIT, Delhi.

Introduction

In the history of industrial accidents, certain names have become imprinted in human mind and Bhopal accident is one of them. This is the worst industrial accident what we have come to know in last 50 years. Such accidents cannot be called as accidents because they were not unseen. From all accounts it appears that Bhopal accident was not caused by unforeseen failure of some highly sophisticated and complex piece of machinery. It was instead a combination of small errors. Post-poned maintenance and poorly trained personnel whose cumulative effect resulted into the ensuing catastrophe.

One would like to take cues from such happenings so that such recurrences could be prevented. Bhopal accident raises a number of basic issues in relation to the industrial hazards. This paper will be dealing with a few basic issues of industrial hazard such as :

(i) Selection of Plant-site,

(ii) the choice of technology,

(iii) the values behind the transfer of technology,

(iv) hazard of lack of communication flow and response; and

(v) the preventive mechanism/measures.

In conclusion some suggestions are given in the paper from the analysis of Bhopal accidents.

(i) First to develop machanisms that would prevent or minimize the occurrence of similar accidents in future ; and

(ii) to cultivate systems for the assessment of responsibility of the various parties involved and to provide a proper kind of administrative mechanisms for the relief of the victims.

The Bhopal accident has raised a number of basic issues in relation to the management of industrial hazards in general and for disaster prevention in developing countries in particular. The more prominent of these are characterized below.

Selection of Plant-Site

Past industrial disaster, including the Mexic City explosion and the Three Mile Island accident, have taught that remote siting provides a major protection against potential calastrophes.

The tragic loss of life at Bhopal was concentrated in the densely populated squallar settlements located within three kilometers of the plant. A remote site for the plant or an exclusion zone of three kilometers at the Union Carbide Plant might have averted most of the fatalities.

One apparent message from Bhopal would call for remote siting of facilities that carry the potential for rare but catastrophic events. Such a policy must be augmented by control over population growth around the facility. Short of truly remote sites. Well-considered locations land use controls can provide important means of disaster minimization.

Bhopal is situated in central India, and the plant site is asside main rail lines leading North to New Delhi. West to Bombay east to Calcutta, and south to the cotton-growing areas near Madras. For Union Carbide, the area was one of the few regions without an electricity shortage, as well, Bhopal's 10-mile-long Upper Lake provided an simple water supply for manufacturing chemicals, and ready pool of labour existed is the city.

Since India has no policy on the sitting of hazardous Industries, no one contested the location of the plant a scant two miles from the center of the city. Although the state department of Town and Country Planning was aware of the plan to manufacture and store MIC, it approved the location and, in preparing the Bhopal Master Plan in 1975, subsequently classified the plant as "general" rather than "obnoxious". This was a grave mistake and which was done knowingly.

Effect of the accident on mental health are acknowledged. Reports of mental trauma and other psychiatic effects, yet there is no systematic programme for monitoring or treating mental health problems. A distinguished group of psychiatrists who visited Bhopal several weeks after the accident acknowledged weakly that people were indeed suffering from anxiety and depression. But it was difficult to attribute these

symptoms to the accident. More recently the King George Medical College has found widespread mental disorders among Bhopal population.

Other damages and burdens add to the human health problems. Some 70,000 to 100,000 persons left the city for distances up to 50 kilometres. This shows that Union Caribide Plant site was not selected properly—it was kept in a densely populated area.

Choice of Technology

Few basic decisions affect hazard potential more than the initial choice of the technology. In the case of Bhopal, the choice involves the long-term storage of MIC, a chemical so extremely hazardous that some countires openly prohibit long-term storage.

The choice-of-technology mistake at Bhopal was not the transfer of the modern formulation plant for bulk pesticides needed for Indian agriculture as many have thought of. Rather it was the construction of such a large MIC-based plant of this particular design, the choice of a particular production process that carried higher inherent risk a catastrophic accident, the choice a scale of plant and equipment (designed to produce 5,000 tons a year) that involved large inventories of highily toxic substances ; and the failure to incorporate technological designs and practices for defence—indepth protection —against major accident.

It the future economic considerations alone should not drive the choice of the imported technology. Rather they should be meticulously balanced with opportunities for risk minimization.

Values behind Transfer of Technology

The Bhopal accident spotlights an inherent tension policies surrounding the transfer of technology to developing countries and in the very nature of complex technologies. The Union Carbide plant came to Bhopal as part of an Indian Plan for self-sufficiency in agricultural production and for Industrialzation of its underdeveloped regions through a labour-intensive technology transfer. But assuring the prevention of catastrophe will probably require tightening controls by parent companies,

which possess the overwhelming capability and knowledge for controlling industrial risks. Regulatary systems, whether in developed or developing countries, will always find it difficult to replicate such resources. Thus the management of catastrophic hazards presses for centralized control by the parent corporation and extensive automation : at the same time, participatory economic development presses for decentralized control indigenous resources development, and labour-intensive production.

Hazard of lack of Communication Flow and Response

Some of the clearest failures in the Bhopal accident involved inadequate information flow and emergency preparedness. These failures occurred at various levels: inadequate understanding of MIC's toxicity and health threat ; lack of knowledge by local government and medical officials of the plant's chemicals and their hazards ; poor information during the accident to guide nearby residents ; and lack of advice to local medical personnel as to recommended treatments.

No public warnings were issued. No information on the movement of the gas cloud broadcast to the factory workers so that people in the vicinity could try to flee to safe directions.

Tragically, people poured out of their homes and ran toward the factory. Although Union Carbide Corporate headquarters sent a telex on December 5, 1984, indicating that victims might be given myal nitrite, sodium nitrite, or sodium thiosuphate if cyanide poisoning (3 possible sequel to MIC exposure) were suspected. UCIL did not divulge to the public, arguing that administration of an antidote for cyanide would create widespread panic. Even basic instructions to breathe through a wet towel, which could have saved the lives of hundreds, were never forthcoming. And this led to various death and ongoing health problem.

Preventive Mechanism and Measures

Behavioural theory tells us that measures of deterrence are effective in modifying both specific and general human behaviour where an element of premeditation is involved in the commitment of crime or socially undesirable behaviour. Where-

as the number of crimes committed during the heat of passion or anger is unlikely to be reduced by incarcerating the alleged perpetrators, corporate decisions are by definition made by management on rational grounds. Therefore, they are more in the nature of crimes of calculation, *i.e.*, risks deliberately taken, and should respond to measures of deterrence that adversely affect those calculations.

(*a*) Safety Measures

One way to minimize potential hazards in manufacturing operations is to incorporate redundant backup safety measures in the plant design to make them as "foolt-proof" as possible. The degree of redundancy required is directly related to the potential risk of accidents from malfunctions or human error caused by insufficient preventive maintenance and poorly trained personnel. It should be mentiond here that this is not a radical notion.

Managements routinely install redundant backup systems where downtime due to plant malfunctions can inflict serious economic costs from loss of production and sales. Therefore, in order to make management of MNCs more cognizant of these risks, their culpability should be determined not on whether they knew of a particular incident, but the extent to which such an incident could or should have been anticipated, and the degree of preventive redundancy that was incorporated into the plant design.

(*b*) Corporate Management Measure

Corporate Management tend to allocate their time and attention to their business in direct proportion to their contribution to a company's overall sales and profits. Union Carbide's Indian operations accounted for a very small portion of its global sales. Therefore, it is not difficult to assume that its top management may not have been fully aware of the company's problems in India.

The accidents in Bhopal, India and at Three Mile Island in the United States, point to another type of risk and associated costs that must receive greater attention from corporate managements and investment communities. To wit, an industrial operation may have a high current return on

investment and a small concurrent risk. However, certain industrial activities carry with them a potential for risk so large as to threaten the very survival of the organization. Therefore, the cost of avoiding such risks, no matter how infrequent the likelihood of their occurrence, must become an integral part of evaluating the economic costs and benefits of such an operation. An increasing awareness of these risks should lead to more prudent decisions on the part of MNCs, both in their plant location and manufacturing operations.

The criterion of measuring a corporation's culpability based on a *post facto* evaluation of preventive actions offers the best prospect for reducing industrial risks in third world countries. This evaluation should embody a corporation's knowledge of the industrial processes involved and its experience in operating in the culture and work environment of these countries.

(c International Measures

It has been suggested that international regulatory mechanisms may be necessary to prevent such accidents. Corporate critics point to the example of the International Code of Breastmilk Substitutes which was enacted by the World Health Organization (WHO) in 1981 to curb allegedly excessive promotional practices of infant formula manufacturers in LDCs. The WHO-Code, however, is the best illustration of the futility and inadequacy of such international regulatory measures.

Instead of mandatory international regulations, an alternative would be to establish minimum and maximum guidelines for safety standards for different types of industrial plants. Each country would have the option of choosing standards within the permissible ranges based on its level of industrial development, safety records, capacity for self-regulation, and economic conditions. To make sure that all countries subscribe to these standards, international loans and exports of high technology equipment should be made conditional to a country's willingness to become a signatory.

Countries and companies choosing safety standards that

are at the upper limit of the permissible range, and those with better records of safety and self-regulation should be rewarded with lower costs of liability insurance. Furthermore, insurance carriers would be the natural instruments for ensuring compliance with prevailing laws and safety regulations. A failure to comply with the standards would result in an increase in the insurance costs, or still worse, unavailability of insurance coverage.

Clearly, a number of measures outlined here would not apply to situations within a single country involving local ownership, with little or no international involvement, and where the government is unwilling or unable to institute appropriate measures of industrial safety. The situation is even worse in many third world countries where the local plant is owned by a state agency and is not subject to external controls and accountability, and where the government's dominant interest lies in greater current production rather than long term safety of workers, or the environment.

Accidents involving citizens of multiple countries invariably get bogged down in jurisdictional disputes, discovering proceedings, and determination of facts. This is so because the manner in which facts are defined and interpreted has a tremendous bearing on the final resolution of a dispute and the allocation of the ultimate financial responsibility. Domestic law courts are, therefore, inappropriate, especially as they relate to multi-country disputes, to establish the questions of fact. These cases can drag on for years while the victims are denied any help at a time when they most need it.

An alternative approach is suggested here. It also involves international cooperation. It is, nevertheless, more flexible and, therefore, more realistic. It has two facets.

One measures would be to develop an international agency that would be staffed by professional experts in different aspects of a accident investigation and damage estimation. This agency would be non-political in nature. Countries would become signatories to the charter of the agency thereby guaranteeing it access to the accident site and other relevant data to facilitate its fact finding function.

A model for such an agency would be the National Transportation Safety Board in the United States, or the International Atomic Energy Agency.

(d) Assessment of Responsibility, Compensation, and Administration of Funds

The issue of compensating the victims of such industrial disasters involves a determination of the size of the compensation pie, the criteria for establishing eligibility and amount of compensation, and above all, responsibility for ensuring that the administration of the compensation system is carried out in an efficient, compassionate, and timely fashion. Having suggested a system of *post facto* evaluation, the question of where such a determination should take place assumes critical importance.

Prior discussions stated the undesirability of using domestic law court systems for the determination of facts, especially as they pertain to accidents involving more than one country. For similar reasons, domestic law courts should not be used for establishing culpability and award levels either. In the case of single country accidents, with no international involvement, the possibility of arbitration should be explored where court procedures may be time consuming and cumbersome.

In the case of international accidents, a more appropriate alternative would be for the World Court to appoint a judicial master who would hear all testimony and ascertain all relevant issues pertaining to the size of the compensation pool, the identification of the parties who should contribute to it, and the definition of eligibility and the appropriate levels of compensation. This approach should drastically reduce legal costs, avoid sensationalism, and provide for a system where both the governments and MNCs are held liable for their negligence and are asked to account for it.

For this system to operate, however, the consent of all the parties is necessary. Normally, the governments of the countries where the MNC is based and where the accident took place would make that commitment. However, in cases where one or the other government is potentially liable for damages it may be reluctant to make such a commitment under

the guise of protecting its sovereignty. Even under those circumstances, it would be highly desirable for one or the other country to seek the findings of a monitor appointed by the International Court because of the weight of world public opinion such findings would carry.

The second factor has to do with the administrative mechanism necessary to manage the compensation system for the benefit of the victims. Remember that in most of the third world countries accident victims are likely to be poor, uneducated, and uninformed. They may not be sophisticated enough to manage large sums of money so that funds would be available to take care of the disabled victims over their life spans which may last anywhere from 1 to 50 years.

A possible approach to this problem could be through the purchase of appropriate annuities guaranteed by internationally reputable insurance carriers. The questions of administration of these funds cannot be left to the sole discretion of the government agencies in LDCs.

Conclusion

In conclusion, let me state that total elimination of serious industrial accidents is impossible regardless of their location. However, growing evidence indicates that their incidence can be greatly reduced given effective monitoring mechanisms, potential for large damage awards, and criminal penalties for corporation and executives found negligent.

This trend is already in evidence in Western Europe and in the United States, and is likely to spread to other parts of the world. It should induce corporations to institute rigorous preventive mechanisms that minimize avoidable financial costs and human misery.

REFERENCES

ABRHAM, MARTIN (1985) : "The Lessons of Bhopal" International Organizations of Consumers Unions, Malaysia.

DELHI SENIOR FORUMS, (1983) : "Bhopal Gas Tragedy", in *Social Scientist* (Kerala) 13, no. 140, 36.

SREEKANT, KHANDEKAR, (1985) : "An Area of Darkness," *India Today*, 30 June 134.

RADHIKA, RAMASESHAN, (1985) : "Bhopal Gas Tragedy : Callousness Abounding," *Economic and Political Weekly*, 20 (12 January), 56-57.

LOIS R. EMBER, (1985) "Technology in India : An Uneasy Balance of Progress and Tradition." *Chemical and Engineering News*, 11 February, p.62.

THOMAS N. GLADWIN, (1985) "The Bhopal Tragedy : Lessons for Management," *NYU Business 5* (*Spring/Summer*) 17-21.

DAVID, DAVIDAR (1985) "Beyond Bhopal ; The Toxic Waste Hazard in India", *AMINO 14*, No. 2, 112-116.

Industry Safety Reforms : Bhopal Inspires New Initiatives," *Chemical and Engineering News*, Ist April, 6.

SETHI, S, PRAKASH (1987) Inhuman Errors," *Columbia Journal of World Business*, Spring ; pp 101-110.

17 | Industrial Counsselling

S. Karunesh*

An employee's effectiveness on his job is influenced greatly by emotional factors relating to his personal life or to his job situations or to both. Sources of stress at home include financial problems, wives or husbands, of sweet hearts, marital discords, in-laws, children, illness, neighbours and so on. At work the employee is subjected to many other stresses. The industrial situation is a constantly changing one. Lay offs occur, men are fined, jobs are changed, production schedules change, fellow employees come and go, opportunities occur for advancement, rivalries develop, *etc.* All this takes place in a setting where men work together for an organization.

Another important factor which determines an employee's functioning on the job is his attitude towards work and these attitudes towards work are sometimes conscious and sometimes unconscious. Many who accept the necessity of working are often unaware that deep down they secretly would be taking care of their work themselves. Various unconscious and conscious feelings about work are often reflected in

* Centre for Management Studies, Indian IIT, Delhi.

behaviour on the job. Some men are always restless and dissatisfied and agitated for change. Others always seem to resist change even though it might be for their own betterment.

Reports indicate from 60 per cent to 80 per cent of all separations or dismissals from the job in industry are due to social incompetence, while 20 per cent to 40 per cent are the result of technical incompetence. Emotional problems affect workers, supervisors, executives, engineers and other all alike. Among the personnel problems which frequently result from emotional factors are the following :

1. Reduced productivity
2. Excessive tardiness and absentees due to illness.
3. Excessive absences for personal reasons other than illness.
4. Antagonism toward regulations and authority.
5. Excessive complaints and grievances.
6. Friction between fellow workers.
7. Withdrawal of individuals from the group.
8. Alcoholism.
9. Accidents.

To deal with these problems managers and supervisors in the organization need to have some knowledge of counselling and to understand industrial counselling they should have some concept of mental health which will give them some guidance. Points by which they will be able to evaluate themselves and others.

Mental health may be defined in many ways. It implies emotional maturity, and a simple definition of emotional maturity is the ability to work, love and play effectively without conflict. Dr. Mauree (1942) gave the following few points for the mental health, they are :

1. Ability to be guided by reality rather than fears.
2. Use of long-term values.
3. Grown up (adult) conscience.
4. Independence.

5. Capacity to 'love' someone else but with an enlightened self-interest.
6. A reasonable dependence.
7. A reasonable aggressiveness.
8. Healthy defence mechanism (self-punishment and blaming others are examples of unhealthy mechanisms).
9. Good sexual adjustment with acceptance of own gender.
10. Good work adjustment.

In some ways it would be ideal if personnel departments could hire only those persons who are completely emotionally mature. Under such circumstances, however, we would probably not have enough workers to run our factories and many workers who are highly productive might be left without jobs. At the time of hiring it is actually very difficult to predict how the prospective employee will function on the job. Certain personality inventory tests are helpful in detecting some applicants with personality disturbances which are potentially more incapacitating, but they require trained personnel to interpret them. Guilford Martin personnel Inventory, and Minnesota Multiphases Personality Inventory and Human Wordsworth test are three well known examples of such tests which are used to measure temperament.

We have talked of mental health, now let us discuss about counselling and how it resolves industrial problems.

The general belief about counselling is giving advice freely from the abundance of your heart ; that people come with problems and the counsellor offers solutions. So anybody can do counselling provided he has a bit of common sense and little experience of life. This is in general the idea of educated people. But counselling in proper sense is different. It is an interpersonal relationship which stimulates growth in the client as a person. Counselling encourages the client to grow in maturity to actualize his potential and to utilize his resources towards definite goals. In this interpersonal relationship two persons are involved—counsellor needs to develop insight into the counselee so that he can solve his own problems.

Now let us discuss some of the genuine problems in indus-

trial settings which managers and supervisors face every now and then and how counselling can help in sorting out these problems.

1. One of the problems more commonly encountered by the supervisor and the manager is the 'touchy' employee who is overly sensitive to any actions or remarks which might reflect upon his worth as a person, his ability or his functioning on his job. These people tend to imagine slights when none are intended, or they magnify or misinterpret or see some special significance in the decisions of the supervisors or the actions of their follow employees. Such individuals are quite insecure and they have an exaggerated need for the approval of others to maintain their self-esteem when such approval is not coming in large doses, they feel rejected. Some become overtly hostile and complain openly, but others do not say anything but instead become withdrawn. They may become inefficient and some may even subtly undermine the effort at hand. These type of individuals require constant reassurance in the process of counselling about their value as persons and of their value to the organizations.
2. Certain employees seem to come to the attention of their supervisors far more often than others. They seem to have more complaints and grievances, more excuses, more special requests, poorer production records, more absence, more differences with their fellow workers and more accidents and they change jobs more often. The pattern for the individual worker varies greatly. Problem workers, such as these, have a variety of emotional conflicts which prevent gratifying their basic needs in healthy ways. Their common characteristics is that they tend to live out their conflicts and express them in their relationships with their environment.

The supervisor and manager of necessity must deal with the overt behaviour, but if they understand that the overt behaviour is the result of the workers unconscious conflicts he is in a

better position to deal with the situation in a constructive manner. 'Problem' workers tend to be very provocative in their behaviour—particularly in their relationships toward authority. The natural tendency of those who are provoked is to retaliate, but retaliation only accentuates the problem. The manager who can recognize that the provocative behaviour is the result of the workers conflict and not a reaction to his personality, will be less threatened by the 'problem' worker. If the manager is patient and a good listener (the basic qualities of the counsellor), he will be able to develop an understanding of the worker which may help the worker or at least the worker's difficulties on the job.

3. Emotional problems are estimated to cause one quarter to one third of the absence from work. Only a small portion of this absenteesm is contributed by employees with disorders that require hospitalization or medical treatment. The bulk of it is due to problems associated with difficulties and dissatisfaction in interpersonal relationships both in the workers outside life and in the job situation.

Studies in reducing absenteeism show that departments with the best developed group solidarity have the lowest rate of absenteeism. Group solidarity is asually associated with a leadership that is basically employee centered. In such groups the worker has a very real sense of belonging. Relationships in such groups tend to provide healthy emotional satisfaction as well as a means for meeting economic needs.

4. Accident proneness : Every observing supervisor/manager is familiar with the fact that certain employees have accidents repeatedly, while others work year after year at similar or even more dangerous jobs with perfect safety records. The same persons as injure themselves repeatedly also seem to have difficulties in other areas. They have more sickness, absenteeism, and they visit dispensaries with minor complaints more often then average employee. They also seem to have more difficulty with their bosses and fellow workers,

and they seem to suffer a disproportionate share of life's misfortunes generally.

To show that accidents do not happen as a matter of chance Dr. Gerald Gordon reported—a study of 3000 occupational injuries occurred over a two year period in a plant showed 100 per cent of the injuries had been incurred by 35 per cent of the total plant population and almost half of these were distributed among a 7 per cent group who had between 2 and 6 injuries each for the two year period. Sixty five cent of the employees had not reported to the dispensary with so much as a scratch. The 7 per cent group of repeaters cannot be accounted for any chance basis.

Among the personality traits commonly mentioned in the literature in relation to accidents and accident proneness are the following :

Aggressiveness, anger, frequent conflict with authority, lack of attention to job at hand, attention getting (show off) tendencies, boredom, tendency to take chances or risks, competitiveness with inability to bear being outdone, discontent, distraction, excitement, guilt feeling, hostility, being in a hurry, impulsiveness, faulty judgement of speed and power, unconscious] need for punishment, unwillingness to accept monotony or routine, neurotic tendencies, being easily offended overt activities, rashness in action, rebelliousness, restlessness and resentments.

5. *Alcoholism* : Industry's interest in alcoholism comes from loss in productivity due to the decreased efficiency and absenteeism that result from excessive drinking. Studies at yale indicate that the use of alcohol causes the problem drinker in industry to miss 22 working days a year. The problem drinker loses an additional to 2 days a year more than other employers for other illness and he has twice the number of accidents. The supervisor together with the plant physician can be of real help to the worker in recognizing the problem as early as possible and in then following through and obtaining assistance from both of these sources.

MANAGERIAL LEADERSHIP WITH COUNSELLING APPROACH

Probably the most important factor contributing to the maintenance of good mental health among the workers in industry is good leadership. Managers/supervisors should be those persons who get along with other people, and they should be persons who have healthy and constructive ways of handling the normal everyday problems of their own lives, he should be persons of above average competence. A manager or supervisor should furthermore have a realistic understanding of his own strengths and limitations both as to the technical aspects of his job and as to his ways of getting along with people. This manager as leader must understand his role in the organization and he must have healthy respect (the another basic quality of the counsellor) for the men who work under him. With the proper respect for all concerned the manager will have a much easier time in exercising the authority which his position demands. If the manager respects the man, if he makes the workers feel that he is accepted and wanted both as a person and as an employee, if he makes the man feel he is capable of doing a better job, the worker will profit. A certain number of failures are inevitable, but the manager can at best have the satisfaction of having tried a constructive approach. Matters of tardiness, absenteeism, rule violations and other disciplinary problems are best handled early when constructive help can remedy the situation rather than late when the problem had advanced to the point where some drastic action is called for.

Conclusion

We may say that problems of mental health which the manager will encounter tend to fall into 3 groups.

1. There is a large group of employees who ordinarily adjust very well, emotionally healthy and mature but under stress and strain in times of crisis need support. The manager at this stage be a great help to these employees just being understanding and by accepting them as friends.

2. There are other employees who have emotional problems or personality disturbance that are significant enough to cause them to be unhappy or uncomfortable or to decrease the

effectiveness in working but they are not in that group which are beyond guidance or professional help. This group actually needs professional counselling. Supervisors can do much by attempting to understand and accept them and by respecting them as individuals who have a contribution to make to their families, their jobs and society at large. If the supervisor is successful in a position to encourage the ones who need counselling, guidance or treatment to seek it. Skill in making original referrals in many cases may determine whether or not the counselling or treatment can be effective. The man who is sent to a counsellor or psychiatric with the feeling that the referral has been made because his supervisors/managers wants to get rid of him has far less chance of profiting by the experience than a man who is referred with the feeling that his supervisor respects him and considers him to have worthwhile potentials and then to be worthy of receiving help.

3. There are third group of people who have emotional illness of such magnitude as to require psychiatric treatment. Too often we condemn these people for being weak as we fail to understand that they are sick. Even some of us who pay lip service to recognize them that they are sick indicate our prejudices by our actions, such people as have recovered often feel quite insecure about the attitudes of others when they first return to work. Supervisors can do much in preparing the other men for their return and helping the others accept them back as members of the group. Former patients do not want to be treated differently.

In industrial counselling supervisor actually should have the quality of a counsellor and for that he needs to develop the art of listening. Being a good listener requires a sincere interest in the other people and patience. If the supervisor is an understanding listener and if he does not feel the compulsion to express his own opinions, the worker may feel comfortable enough to talk about what is actually bothering him.

Listening is of value because it offers the speakers an opportunity for emotional catharsis or ventilation, but it does have its limitations when working with persons with deep emotional problems. If the problems which the worker presents gets worse than instead of better, if they

become more frequent, or if the worker seems to get no benefit from talking about his problems or becomes more upset, it is time to refer them to specialize trained counsellor. The plant medical department or personnel office should have counselling cell with trained professional counsellor to deal with these type of emotional problems.

REFERENCES

1. FRITZ, REDLICH *et al* (1953) *The Inside Story: Psychiatry and Everyday Life*, Alfred A. Knopf, New York, pp. 46.
2. FUSTER, J.M. *Helping in Personal Growth : A New Approach to Counselling*, St. Paul Publication.
3. GERALD, GORDON, M.D. (1954) 'The People who get hurt', *Safety News*, Vol. 69, No. 2 February, p. 20.
4. HARRY, LEVINSON (1955) "Consultation Clinic for Alcoholism" *Menninger Quarterly*, Winter Issue, p. 15.
5. JAMES, A, DIRKHOOD, (1953) "The mind behind the accident" *Safety News*, Vol 68, No. 6 December.
6. LEONARD,E. HIMLER, (1954) "Psychological Factors in Industrial Accidents", *Michigan Business Review*, Vol. VI, No. 2, March, p. 12.
7. STEPHEN, MURGAT ROYD, "Counselling and helping" *Psychology in Action*, The British Psychological Society and Methuen, London and New York.
8. RUSSEL, FRASER; (1947) "Incidence of Neurosis among Factory Workers", *Medical Research Council Industrial Health Research Board Report* 90, H.M. Stationers Office, London, p. 4.
9. SPRIEGL, SCHULTZ AND SPRIEGEL, *Elements of Supervision*, Wiley Int. Edition.
10. WILLIAM C. MENNINGER, *What makes an Effective Man?* American Management Association, Personnel Series No. 152, p. 24.
11. —— 1951 "Self Understanding" Better Living Booklet, Science Research Associates, Chicago, p. 48.

18 Computer Systems within the Psycho-Social Framework

Anuradha Sharma*

Computer systems are being successfully used as tool for data analysis and information storage in almost all branches of science. However the social, psychological and ethical issues remain challenges for computer system designers and planners. These issues are basically related to the nature of man and the conflicting technological and humanistic values in society. The assumption here is that technology is essentially neutral and the results depend entirely on the decisions to make use of a particular technology,

It is, therefore, important that the computer technology moves in a direction which has to produce human as well as the technical gains for society. For such a philosophy, the computer systems should be designed with a vision of man where alternative ways of making technological choices in terms of human psychological needs must be made. The work designs should not be technologically deterministic, but should permit job satisfaction, job enrichment and motivation of the

* Department of Humanities and Social Sciences, I.I.T. Delhi.

user. Newer computer system designs therefore need to consider social changes and human aspirations along with technological changes. There has to be a partnership between the man and the machine. Computer as a mataphor is yet another social responsibility of scientists. The artificial intelligence revolution may develop minds even superior to man. The question, however, is whether we need few 'great minds' or all minds. Through a 'science fiction vision' one may feel that the greatest potentials of mankind, *i.e.*, decision-making and reasoning almost disappear. One wonders what will happen to freshness of ideas and creativity given to man by nature and how to manage those ideas which computers may generate. In addition to these, the psychological fear may increase and identity, achievement, growth, emotion, love and belongingness may suffer. Perhaps new strategies of time management and new life styles will emerge as a result of computer functions. This may give rise to dysfunctional energy in society. These extra-ordinary implications for society need to be considered in planning. Since we cannot lag behind other countries in developments, we must enter the 'computer age'. However, scientists, technologists and planners must design systems with social responsibility. The great potentials of computer technology must be designed and used within the psycho-social framework. This paper is addressed to highlight such issues through socio-technical perspective, work psychology and quality of life concepts,

In the analysis of 'computer systems within the psycho-social framework', the socio-technical systems perspective becomes important. This approach emphasises on the relationship of technology to people as a key factor in the effectiveness systems. The socio-psychological effects of technology, the relationship of newer work systems and people, adjustment to new technology and management of change become important considerations in this regard. The resulting social revolution as a result of new technologies is thus extremely important while anthropologist Leslie observes in this context that social systems are in a very real sense secondary and subsidiary to technological system. Technology is the independent variable and social system the dependent variable. Thus there is a

conditioning process going on.

Work, worker and working are undergoing tremendous change today. Perhaps the changes today are significantly greater than any time since the industrial revolution. In recent years science and technology have played a significant role in shaping social cultural and individual aspirations particulary work psychology of workers in organizations.

Challenges of computerization for work psychology are enormous. Like any other new technology computer technology also requires more individual commitment and autonomous work designs. It also increases the dependence of the organization on individuals. Therefore, manifestation of psycho-social effects and degree of these effect need to be considered in system designs. Choices available on the psycho-social assumption make it possible to design humane systems. Rapidly changing technological imputs result in massive dislocations at times. It gives rise to crisis in social values and calls for a high degree of adaptation mechanism.

Computerization as a correlate of quality of life is extremely important. The main consideration in any technological knowledge and development has to be elimination of poverty and offering superior quality of life and quality of working life for people. Even though it is observed and recognized by many people that technological foundations of economic growth and intellectual cultures are important, there seems to be a feeling that technology often sets conditions of subordination and sets limits to human values cherished by societies. Perhaps this is the prime danger that mankind faces today. Technology is important but perhaps this is not the only cause of rise and fall of civilization.

Quality of working life is a normative concept. It takes into its definition factors like achievement, recognition, autonomy and creativity on the job. Davis and Taylor observe that advanced technology provides not an automatically enhanced quality of working life but a new opportunity. They attack the technological determinism on the ground that technology was not pre-determined by its own interest, logic and developmental 'Laws' but in substantial part by the psycho-social assumptions. According to Tom Forester (1989) there

many different types of determinism. For example there is the determinism that sees technology as a cause of social change and determinism that sees-technology as a consequence of social change. However, in the present context the system of Technology and Social change appear cyclical in nature and need careful consideration.

The changes in work design to computerization call for greater group cooperation and cordination, free and all channel communication, more involvement and commitment of workers. Ergonomic considerations need to be incorporated in such work designs. User interface and the issues of management of change need further analysis in this context. This high-tech development must not snatch away the creativity of human minds.

We have now entered the computer age in a big way, through planning and allocation of huge funds, through schools, through consumer movements, through industrial production and in many other ways. However, there is scarcity of ideas, concerns data and analysis of its social organizational and individual correlates. Concerns for social conseqences of technologies, particularly computer technology is a social responsibility and must be included in the curriculum design of higher learning institutions.

19 | Perspectives on Social Responsibility of Managers

Anuradha Sharma* and Raka Sharan*

Managers tend to look at social responsibility as a fringe activity and often give non-serious consideration to this aspect. The concept, however, is equally important in the intangible areas like management styles and services sectors. Some aspects of this concern were highlighted by speakers in the workshop on social responsibilities. The views expressed are presented in this chapter to enhance our insights about social responsibilities of managerial roles. The issues summarized here deal with multiple roles of engineering professionals, managerial communication, quality of life and quality of work life, management of change, promotion of researches and academic administration, public systems methodology and social responsibility of legal profession.

Multiple roles of engineering professionals may be viewed as economists, planners, advisors, managerials, entrepreneurs, teachers, researchers and consultants as analysed by Prof. Agrawal. Therefore, a manager engineer has social responsibility of playing these roles effectively.

Managerial Communication as a social responsibility is

*Departments of Humanities and Social Sciences, IIS Delhi,

highlighted by Dr. Amulya Khurana. She said that about 30 years ago a typical manager was not aware of the implications and significance of communication in organisation and he did not bother about this aspect. But today's manager recognises that "communication" is probably his most important responsibility. In order to coordinate organisational activities managers spend a great deal of their time interacting with other people. Therefore, communication skills and an understanding of the managerial communication process become increasingly more important to the managers all the time.

Generally communication means exchange of thoughts, information, facts, ideas, openings, feelings or emotions by two or more persons to bring about mutual understanding, confidence of human relations. The purpose of communication is usually to effect change or influence actions.

Effective communication is a basic prerequisite for attainment of organisational goals. It is beyond doubt that good management requires the manager to have good communication skills. In addition to his essential responsibilities of providing proper leadership, planning, controlling, decision-making and giving careful attention to workers' moral, the manager has another important duty ; that is, to create adequate eonditions for effective communication, because, communication, is as vital to an organisation as the blood stream to a person.

Emphasizing the responsibility in terms of quality of life and quality of work by Dr. Banwet said ; two relatives represent the quality of our life – Power of money and Power of values. A manager wherever he might be working his work environment could constitute economic environment, technological environment, social environment, political and legal environment and ethical environment. It is this ethical environment which leads to the notion of social responsibility of managers.

The quality of life and the quality of work life is vastly affected by this environment. Work has impact on environment and environment has an impact on the work organisation. Quite a few ecological disbalances are caused by us.

Stressing the 'Management of change' Mr. Arumugham

said that energy plays an important role in the National economic development. Energy touches the life of each and every citizen in different sectors. There are competing forms of Energy—some yet to be developed for a more massive application. The criteria governing the managerial attitude and the entrepreneurial objectives of technologists and organisations need to be developed. What should be these criteria ? What should be the dynamics of change in these criteria ?

Other responsible areas relate to the quality of products and services which are the results of activities and advancements by Scientists and Technologists. The focus on satisfying the customer brings out a different approach to Organisation and Management. When "Quality First—Not Profit First" becomes the credo, a totally new line of Human Resources and Infra-structure development emerges. Participative Management becomes valuable, not just as a desirable Industrial Relations but as a necessary ingredient of Management, oriented towards fulfilling the objectives of the organization. Participative Management ceases to be one of sharing the Management Power at the top but becomes one of delegating responsibility for Management down to all levels. The social consequences of such Participative Management are the elements of Industial Democracy about which Indian Scientists and Technologists have to learn considerably more, assimilate extensively and practice routinely.

Change is inherent in the development of Science and Technology. Society, consequently, is faced with change. Who are the change Masters? How do they steer change so that stable organizations emerge ? Let us think.

Social Responsibility from the Angle of Research Highlighted on the Concept and Development

India possesses the second largest quantum of technical manpower in the world. In spite of this, India continues to remain one of the poorest countries in the world. The causes of overall poor performance according to him are that people have a tendency for not working, people want secured jobs, there is lot of corruption in the country, compensation for technical jobs is inadequate, our Economy is a high cost Economy, and

Indian population is growing at a rapid rate. However, all these observations as causes of poof performance of the economy may be summarised by one word, that is, "Mismanament". In the Indian context, mismanagement is applicable to the whole economy as well as its various sub-sectors and segments. The present need of the nation is to develop and utilise its human resources effectively.

The R&D institutions should, therefore, be managed with the objective of promotion of nationally research. For this, RMIS (Research Management Information System) should be developed. To enable the researchers to devote their maximum time for research, administrative system of R&D institutions should be modified accordingly. The system of selection of potential and talented researchers also needs a thorough change. It is only a strong feeling of social responsibility that can bring about such changes.

Social Responsibilities of Managements have also to be viewed through Legal Profession Perspective

By legal profession here we mean all such persons by whatever name called, whose calling it is to be a specialist in and/or a practitioner of law, whether enrolled or not. Thus the term includes an advocate, attorney, barrister, counsellor, consultant, mukhtar, pleader, solicitor and vakil.

Social responsibility is not confined to adherence to the code of professional ethics, it rather encompasses efforts to meet the general and particular expectations of the society at large from a legal professional both in the latter's capacity as an ordinary citizen and as a lawyer-citizen. The concept of social responsibility itself, in this sense, is new, as yet evolving and dynamic especially in respect of the intangible service sector.

Article 51A of the Constitution of India enumerates and formalises the expectations of the Indian society from us, the ordinary citizens ; that whether these duties were hand-picked out of those that stood out as the guiding factors during the three decades of our independence (1947-76) or were those pitiably conspicuous by their absence, is not a subject of this paper.

The code of professional conduct and etiquette for the legal profession has been statutorily sanctified under the Part VI, Chapter II of the Bar Council of India Rules framed under the Advocates Act, 1961. These edicts have been codified under the sub-heads : Duty to the Court, Duty to the Client, Duty to Opponent, Duty to Colleagues, Duty in Imparting Training and Duty to Render Legal Aid.

Since we follow the system of common law (in opposition to civil law) the statutory codes augmented/refined by judgement law. Hence, the courts have been called upon to answer and have answered, as to whether the organised Bar can resolve not to serve a class of litigants or a particular litigant. The courts have also dwelt upon the questions whether a lawyer owes 'duty of care', like any other skilled professional, to his client, and whether the aggrieved client can sue him for punitive/compensatory reliefs under the law of torts, Indian contract Act, 1872, or Specific Relief Act, 1963. Some of the newest forums for seeking relief are those established/authorised under the Monopolies and Restrictive Trade Practices Act, 1969 (in respect of 'unfair trade practices') and the Consumer Protection Act, 1986 (yet to come into force even after the lapse of more than one year).

However, it is in his capacity of a lawyer-citizen that a legal practitioner faces an as yet uncharted or only partially charted route. In this capacity one of his foremost duties is to provide free/concessional legal aid advice, and equally important its to render it fearlessly in deserving/specific cases. This broad field of responsibility may be divided into the following four classifications, for expediency :

(a) Free legal aid to the indigent persons : Besides the passing of the Legal Services Authorities Act, 1987, the Government of India, as enjoined by Articles 39A of the Constitution, has been providing free legal aid and advice to the needy for about eight years now under the auspices of the Committee for Implementing Legal Aid Schemes (Ministry of Law and Justice). In addition, numerous voluntary bodies have come up to

give legal aid and advice to the poor, *e.g.* Indian Council of Legal Aid and Advice.

(b) Persons of moderate means who for want of adequate financial wherewithal, lose out to such adversaries as can afford to engage more competent counsels in a necessarily 'adversary litigative process'. Though the Government has recently taken some initiative in this area by way of establishing *Lok Adalata*, the individual lawyers have had accommodated such clients from time to time; even otherwise legal services are not provided on strict *quid pro quo*-basis. An area that can be gainfully exploited is socio-legal insurance, amongst others, *e.g.* full-time attorneys and para legal personnel on Govt. pay roll.

(c) Persons whose cause a man of ordinary tenacity is scared to espouse, *e.g.* those taking up a cause against powerful and influential persons or against a member of the bar or a person charged with committing a heinous crime.

(d) Causes for which the legal practitioners have a special competence and insight because of their special training and experience, to assure limited social leadership; in fact, every calling has this duty towards contemporaneous society, be it the profession of engineers, doctors, academicians, and the like; in other words, the causes which have come to be known in India as 'public interest litigation'. Though the precursor of this movement can be traced to the USA, yet it must be admitted in fairness that such a movement could not have taken root in the alien Indian soil but for the vision and tenacity of purpose of certain learned judges belonging to the activist (non-textual model) and the creative models like the former Chief Justice P.N. Bhagwati; and equally must we not forget the contributions made by public-spirited men, including the members of the Bar. To sum up, it may be emphasised that the prime responsibility of the legal profession, in the present socio-political, economic and legal context, is to make their brethren aware of

> their rights in the backdrop of the true meaning of the powerful word 'freedom' so that a proper environment could be conceived, debated and established in which the best in the society could be brought out, promoted and sustained. In this direction the legal profession must not shirk its duty to assume limited leadership role.

In recent years systems methodology has been developed for analysing various concepts ; Dr. M.C. Mathur observed that, it is our belief that an engineer interacts with the society through design and operation of those system. In fact engineer's actions in dealing with public systems result in direct interactions with the society. The mathematico-theoretic framework in which the engineer is trained is so much ingrained in his approach that finds no scope of humans in his designs and analysis of any system. Expectations in terms of his 'social responsibility' from such an engineer is, something, of which he is totally ignorant.

By their very nature the public systems are very large and complex systems. In the systems engineering terminology these are termed as real-world systems. How they impinge upon society and over a period how social change is brought about is the subject matter of Technological Forecasting and Assessment. This topic and many which deal with public systems, which when put together from a body of literature called 'public systems methodology', are going to be talked about briefly.